Great
Journey

The Glorious Journey

A reflection book based on

THE TWO POPES

LIAM KELLY

DARTON · LONGMAN + TODD

First published in 2020 by
Darton, Longman and Todd Ltd
1 Spencer Court
140–142 Wandsworth High Street
London SW18 4JJ

Print book ISBN: 978-0-232-53493-1
Ebook ISBN: 978-0-232-53494-8

A catalogue record for this book is available from the British
Library.

Designed and produced by Judy Linard
Printed and bound in Great Britain by Bell & Bain, Glasgow

Contents

Introduction

1978 was 'The Year of the Three Popes': Pope Paul VI died on 6 August, John Paul I was elected on 26 August, but died 33 days later; and John Paul II was elected on 16 October.

2020 brought us 'The Year of the Four Popes' – at least to our screens. John Malkovich starred as Pope John Paul III and Jude Law as Pope Pius XIII in the drama television series *The New Pope*, while Jonathan Pryce appeared as Pope Francis and Anthony Hopkins as Pope Benedict XVI in the bromance comedy *The Two Popes* – for a Church used to one pope at a time, things were confusing!

Pope Francis and Pope Benedict XVI are remarkable figures. They are newsworthy and they fill column inches, even if – perhaps inevitably – those column inches tend to focus on supposed divisions in today's Church. Headlines like 'Dueling Popes', 'Pope vs. Pope', 'Two Popes and One Big Furor' are not uncommon. The presence of two popes at the same time in the Vatican is certainly historic.

The Two Popes film is not historical fact, but the Church on the silver screen. It is a papal biopic, a biographical, bromance comedy. It is cinema, and in watching the film there are times when the 'All persons fictitious' disclaimer comes to mind: 'This is a work of fiction. Any resemblance to actual events or locales or persons, living or dead, is entirely coincidental.'

But in reality *The Two Popes* is a mixture of fact, fiction, and artistic license (and error, too!), inspired by true events. The author of the original book and play on which the film is based, Anthony McCarten, was inspired to write while standing in St Peter's Square watching Pope Francis celebrate Mass, while a few hundred yards away Pope Benedict XVI was living in his residence behind the Basilica: 'Two popes, then, within a solid stone's throw of each other!'[1]

Much of the film centres around an extended conversation between Pope Benedict XVI and Cardinal Jorge Bergoglio, on the occasion of the latter's visit to the Vatican to discuss his retirement. While it is true that bishops are obliged to submit their resignation when they reach 75 years of age, this does not necessitate a personal visit to the pope. What the viewer sees in *The Two*

[1] Anthony McCarten, *The Two Popes* (New York, Flatiron Books, 2019), p. xxii.

Popes is, at best, a dramatic, artistic recreation and interpretation of fact. A number of legitimate questions might come to mind: did the two men really hear each other's confession? Who really knew in advance about Pope Benedict's decision to resign? Vatican media experts – Vaticanologists – suggest the pope only told his personal secretary, Monsignor Georg Gänswein, his brother, Father Georg Ratzinger, and the then Dean of the College of Cardinals, Cardinal Angelo Sodano. Monsignor Alfred Xureb, also a personal secretary to Benedict XVI, has said the pope informed him of his plan to resign just six days before the announcement. Did Pope Francis and Pope Benedict XVI really sit down together to watch the 2014 World Cup Final between Argentina and Germany? As McCarten said, 'What you always do is you speculate. Hopefully, that speculation is based in facts and the truth, and hopefully it's inspired.'[2]

The purpose of this book, however, is not to provide a film review. Many experts far more qualified than me have expressed their own views about the merits of the film as a whole and specific elements within it, even trying to answer such all-important questions, for example, as whether Pope Benedict XVI really likes Fanta!

[2] Quoted in Steve Pond, 'The Two Popes', *The Wrap* magazine, December 2019, p. 55.

I will state, though, that I think it is a good film. Yes, I know you can quibble about whether Anthony Hopkins really has the right physique to play the fragile nonagenarian Benedict XVI; whether one of Benedict's favourite TV programmes really was an Austrian TV police drama *Kommisar Rex*, starring a crime-fighting police dog (might this be a joke, given the media portrayal of Pope Benedict XVI as 'God's Rottweiler'?). You might also notice that some of the chronology is wrong, with things that occurred after the election of Pope Francis depicted as taking place in the papacy of Benedict XVI; or you might rail at a conservative vs. liberal agenda mirroring media stereotypes (and largely mirrored in the film reviews written by pro-Francis and pro-Benedict supporters).

But none of this is the point. I believe the great merit of this film is its ability to place theological discussion in a piece of popular entertainment. Two men, who happen to be religious figures, explore a number of themes which are at the heart of being human, of faith and belief: guilt, forgiveness, mercy, loneliness, suffering, service, leadership. *The Two Popes* is not about Pope Francis and Pope Benedict XVI. It is not good pope vs. bad pope. Even though the film appears to be somewhat pro-Francis, it is Benedict who actually gets some of the best lines. When

INTRODUCTION

Bergoglio claims he is often mis-quoted by the media or his words taken out of context, Benedict advises him to tell the newspapers the opposite of what he thinks: 'Your chances of being quoted correctly might therefore improve!'; or one of the best lines of the film, when Bergoglio says that he does not see the joke in Pope Benedict's quip about 1978 being the year when there were three popes, leading to the great riposte from the German pope that it was '... a German joke. It doesn't have to be funny.'

In essence, *The Two Popes* is an exploration of universal human values. Fundamentally, it is an analysis of human nature.

I am not asking the reader to take sides, but to stop, to reflect and to listen. When Anthony McCarten was standing in St Peter's Square he was wondering when the last time was that there were two popes: he found the answer via Google on a smartphone. The ubiquitous mobile phone! Today we live in a world characterised by its interconnectedness and busy-ness. People spend an average of three hours and 15 minutes on their phones every day and pick up their phones an average of 58 times a day. This book is an invitation, a chance to put down the phone, even switch it off!

The Old Testament book of Ecclesiastes,

written around 3,000 years ago, tells us that there is 'a season for everything, a time for every occupation under heaven', including a time to keep silent (Ecclesiastes 3:1). In 1984, the German film director Philip Gröning asked the Carthusian monks of the Grande Chartreuse, a monastery in the French Alps, if he could film a documentary about the everyday lives of Carthusian monks. The monks, who live an austere life of silence, said they wanted time to think about it. Sixteen years later they let Gröning know they agreed to his proposal. The fruit of Gröning's work, entitled *Into Great Silence*, is just over two-and-a-half hours watching the monks go about their daily business in total silence – no sound effects, no dialogue, no voice-overs, just occasional scriptural subtitles. It is almost a retreat experience on the big screen, inviting the viewer not just to watch, but also to think, even to immerse themselves in the experience.

The Glorious Journey provides an opportunity to watch and think, to read and reflect. The Netflix website says *The Two Popes* is 'cerebral, heartfelt, witty'. So sit back, relax, open your heart and mind and enjoy the film ... and the book!

How to use this book

Six themes have been chosen which, through the lens of popular entertainment, provide a catalyst for personal and group reflection. Although they are taken from the film, they are not, of course, exclusive to the film, and so other sources for reflection, other ideas and suggestions are also included.

The book can be read individually or used as part of a group discussion. It is important to bear in mind that any discussion in a group setting should be founded on respect and sensitivity, it should not become a dialogue of the deaf or even less a shouting-match. Honesty, openness, a willingness to listen and learn can lead to fruitful dialogue. Throughout the text there are questions for reflection and, if you are in a group, for sharing (if you wish – no one should be forced to speak). The questions are not about making sure you get the right answers – it is not an exam. They are there simply to stimulate thought and reflection.

What if you haven't seen *The Two Popes*? This book picks up on themes in the film. It will help if you have seen the film, and even better if you can see clips while reading this book since the different media – the printed word, the visual imagery, the audio – can all play their part in stimulating reflection. But if that is not possible the book should still provide some food for thought – at least that's the challenge laid down for the author!

Ground rules for groups
- Speak if you want to, not because you feel you have to
- Say what you want, not what you think others might want to hear
- Listen with respect to the contributions of others
- Respect the confidentiality of the group so that it is a safe place to be honest.

The Journey

Watch the opening scene of *The Two Popes* set in Buenos Aires.

(4 minutes)

'Any journey, no matter how long, has to start somewhere. Any journey, no matter how glorious, can start with a mistake. So when you feel lost, don't worry. God will not give up.'

Cardinal Bergoglio

The late Cardinal Cormac Murphy-O'Connor, Archbishop of Westminster from 2000-2009, occasionally included in his homilies a joke about a stranger asking a local for directions to a specific place. 'Well, sir,' the reply began, 'if I were you I wouldn't be starting from here.'

St John Paul II was no stranger to travel. In the course of his pontificate 'The Travelling Pope' clocked up more than 750,000 miles, equivalent to more than 28 times the circumference of the earth, or three times the distance from the Earth to the Moon. On all papal journeys the back seats of the papal plane are occupied by the Vatican Accredited Media Personnel, or, to give them their popular acronym, the V.A.M.P.s.

I don't think the VAMPs ever asked the pope, 'Are we there yet?', but I'm sure parents taking their children on holidays will have heard, perhaps on innumerable occasions, such a lament from the back of the car. When I was a child summer holidays were spent in Ireland, and mum or dad, neither of whom could drive, would take their excited children on the long train journey. From home in Derby to Crewe, Crewe to Holyhead, boat to Dun Laoghaire, another train to Dublin, and then the Westport train down to the West of Ireland. Fifty years ago we had no smartphones, X-boxes or gadgets to pass the time on that long journey. 'I-spy' quickly became boring, so the ultimate competition for us sports-mad children was who could spot the most football stadium floodlights from the train! We were excited children, definitely noisy scamps (there were no Quiet Carriages in those days, either) and certainly not VAMPs!

- What are your recollections of childhood journeys, or journeys on which you have taken your own children?
- What were the highlights of those journeys?

- 'Any journey, no matter how long, has to start somewhere. Any journey, no matter how glorious, can start with a mistake.' What do you think Cardinal Bergoglio meant?

Pope Francis's first trip abroad after his election to the papacy was to Brazil to celebrate World Youth Day in July 2013. One image from that trip went viral: the pope boarding the plane in Rome carrying his own hand-luggage, a black briefcase. He never let anyone else carry it and on the way back from Brazil during the in-flight press conference with the VAMPs one of the first questions was 'What's in the briefcase?' The pope assured the VAMPs that it didn't contain the key for the atom bomb! 'When I travel I take it,' he said. 'Inside I have a razor, prayer book, a notebook, and a book to read.' The pope went on to explain that he was surprised that the image had gone viral, because he was just being normal. 'We must get used to being normal. The normality of life,' he said.

Going on a journey, being on a journey, is so normal, and the cliché of life as a journey has become normal, too. Every journey must have a starting-point. This is not simply about when all the suitcases are packed, or even when the pope has put his briefcase in the overhead locker and fastened his seatbelt. It is far more profound than that: 'Before I formed you in the womb I knew you; before you were born I consecrated you' (Jer. 1:5).

Our journey in life began long before we joined it at a particular moment in time. In the words addressed to the prophet Jeremiah, God is indicating that God has created the path along which we are called before we know it. The Old Testament is full of stories of individuals who have set out on a journey. In chapter 12 of the Book of Genesis, Yahweh addresses Abram: 'Leave your country, your kindred and your father's house for a country that I shall show you' (Gen. 12:1). Some people might call this blind faith on the part of Abram, others great trust, while modern-day parlance would probably talk about Abram being called out of his comfort zone, to leave his safe surroundings and go to a place he did not know.

For most of us, the journeys we undertake have the comfort of a starting-point and an end-point, a departure and an arrival, getting from A to B. Abram, without the technological comfort of a SatNav to guide him or prior knowledge from TripAdvisor to give him the low-down on his destination, was simply being asked to trust the one who promised him 'a country that I shall show you.' In the New Testament, that desire for certainty and security which we all crave is stated clearly by Thomas, who says to Jesus, 'Lord, we do not know where you are going; how can we know the way?' (John 14:5).

Thomas's words encapsulate perfectly the confusion, the different interpretations about the word 'journey': Thomas is talking about a journey as going from place to place, like our holiday trips to the West of Ireland, or the many papal journeys of Saint Pope John Paul II, Pope Benedict XVI and Pope Francis. But the words ascribed to Cardinal Bergoglio in *The Two Popes*, the call of Abram, and Jesus' response to Thomas – that he is the Way, the Truth, and the Life – are surely about a different journey: the journey of faith. 'Any journey, no matter how long, has to start somewhere.' In religious terminology, the journey is usually termed our pilgrimage through life. There is a destination – eternal life – but there are many twists and turns along the road.

- What does the idea of faith as a journey mean to you?
- 'So when you feel lost, don't worry. God will not give up.' Are there times when you feel lost, when you feel God has been absent?
- 'I am the Way; I am Truth and Life' (John 14:6). How might these words provide hope?

In the run-up to the conclave that elected Pope Francis, the Vatican Press Office gave detailed descriptions of the measures being taken to maintain the secrecy and confidentiality of the whole process. The cardinals are sworn to secrecy and any cardinal violating the oath sworn at the start of the conclave is automatically excommunicated. There is no access to newspapers, TV, no mobile phones, no Wi-Fi. Even the windows of each room in the Domus Sancta Marthae, where the cardinals reside, are sealed. The Sistine Chapel is swept with electronic devices to ensure there are no bugging devices or hidden cameras. Part of the beautiful, colourful mosaic floor is covered by a false, raised wooden floor beneath which are hidden jamming devices to prevent listening devices, mobile phones, and bugs from working in the chapel. But despite all the state-of-the-art security, within weeks media reports listed how many votes the different cardinals had received. So much for a secret process carrying the threat of automatic excommunication.

Even though we know the outcome, some of the dramatic tension in *The Two Popes* revolves around the casting and counting of votes during the conclave. The voting rules state that on the ballot sheet each cardinal must write legibly, in handwriting that cannot be identified as his, the name of the person he chooses. The votes are read out: 'Bergoglio – Bergoglio – Ratzinger – Ratzinger – Bergoglio ...' In 2005 and 2013 the person elected did not want the role to which they had been called. On the balcony of St Peter's Basilica on 19 April 2005, Pope Benedict XVI said that the fact that the Lord 'knows how to work and to act even with inadequate instruments comforts me', and a few days later he spoke of a feeling of 'human powerlessness as I face the lofty task that awaits me'. Pope Benedict XVI was even more honest speaking to German pilgrims who had come to Rome for the inauguration of his pontificate: 'When, little by little, the trend of the voting led me to understand that, to say it simply, the axe was going to fall on me, my head began to spin.' As for Pope Francis, he was quite blunt with the cardinals: 'May God forgive you for what you have done!'

The papal election is almost a dramatic statement of a well-known passage from the prophet Isaiah: 'Do not be afraid for I have redeemed you; I have called you by your name, you are mine' (Isa. 43:1). The journey of faith is not an anonymous one, for it is a journey along which God has called each one of us by name. It may not be to the burden of the papacy (fortunately!), but just like the pope each one of us is called by name. That calling is celebrated when we are baptised, given a name and welcomed into God's family. The Church believes that through baptism we become part of the family of the Church forever. Baptism leaves an indelible mark. There may be a time when we may choose to walk away from the Church or God, but God will never turn away from us, and will always call us by name. The world of modern technology has now impacted on this, too, and some people who have renounced the Church have asked that their baptism records be deleted under General Data Protection Regulations (GDPR). Perhaps a case of called by name, deleted by technology.

The *Rite of Baptism* in the Catholic Church is in fact meant to be a symbolic representation of the journey of life and faith, the journey on which the baptised person has been called. The ceremony may begin at the door of the church, a simple and effective way of expressing the idea that baptism is the way into the Church and the door to life in Christ. The parents announce the name of their child, and the priest says 'N., the Christian community welcomes you with great joy.' The journey is not a solitary one, but one undertaken within a community.

The ceremony then moves into the church to hear Scripture readings, for the journey in life is guided by the Word of God. The baptism itself takes place in the baptistery or at the baptismal font, and the final stage of the ceremony takes place at the sanctuary or altar, for this is where the other sacraments of Christian initiation – Confirmation and the Eucharist – will be celebrated. The celebration of baptism can be a strong, symbolic representation of the journey of faith on which the baptised person has been called by name.

'Any journey, no matter how glorious, can start with a mistake,' said Cardinal Bergoglio in *The Two Popes*. The journey of life is full of mistakes, for we are all sinners. St Augustine of Hippo (354-430) wrote: 'Sin is energy in the wrong channel.' The journey which started at baptism is a calling to pursue a particular path in life, to go down a particular route. 'We are ambassadors for Christ,' St Paul wrote to the people of Corinth (2 Cor. 5:20). And yet it is in our sinful state that Christ continues to call us. 'And indeed I came to call not the righteous, but sinners' (Matt. 9:13).

In our busy, even frenetic world it is easy to spend a lot of time at meetings, thinking about setting and measuring targets, Key Performance Indicators (KPIs), milestones, and the direction of travel. Of course, there are usually consequences for those who do not meet their KPIs or who set off in a different direction. How different this is from the Gospel, from the journey of faith. I am a sinner, I am certainly not on the path to sainthood. In business jargon, my direction of travel may often be at odds with the direction along which I was called at baptism. And yet Jesus loves me. Still calling.

The parable of the prodigal son in Luke's gospel is very well-known. It is not uncommon to hear preachers asking the congregation to consider whether they are more like the younger or the older son. But it is easy to overlook what I think is the key sentence: 'while he was still a long way off, his father saw him' (Luke 15:20). Not only was he looking out for him, he then rushed to meet him, put his arms around him and kissed him, kissed the son who, by asking for his share of the estate, was in effect saying that his father was more use to him dead than alive. And this is all before the prodigal son had a chance to begin his well-rehearsed explanation of what had happened. The enormity of that is astonishing: to love someone whose words and actions suggest they think you are more use dead than alive.

It is easy to use the phrase 'unconditional love' and apply it to the love shown by the father in this parable. But the enormity of what it really means is far more difficult to comprehend. In the parable of the prodigal son it could be argued that the least the younger son owes his father is an apology, and perhaps an apology to his brother, too, for leaving him to do all the work. But the father loves him so much he just wants him to know that. Whatever wretched state he was in, no matter bad he might have felt about what he had done while he was away, the father was looking out for him. He rushed to meet him. The younger son was a failure, but that did not lessen the father's love.

Pope Benedict XVI has compared the stages of this parable to the stages in each person's journey in their relationship with God.

There can be a phase that resembles childhood: religion prompted by need, by dependence. As man grows up and becomes emancipated, he wants to liberate himself from this submission and become free and adult, able to organise himself and make his own decisions, even thinking he can do without God. Precisely this stage is delicate and can lead to atheism, yet even this frequently conceals the need to discover God's true Face. Fortunately for us, God never fails in his faithfulness and even if we distance ourselves and get lost he continues to follow us with his love, forgiving our errors and speaking to our conscience from within in order to call us back to him.[3]

I, too, am a sinful failure, but the very sort of person still being called by name, by the loving Father. The mistakes we make in life, the sins we commit, can weigh down upon us, can be a real burden. There may be times, too, when things just seem too difficult, when life itself is a dark, troublesome place. In *The Two Popes* Cardinal Bergoglio says God 'will not give up'. Years ago a popular poster and prayer card in religious bookshops depicted a set of footprints in the sand. The poem *Footprints* is about faith and perseverance. The set of footprints depict the Lord accompanying the individual along the journey of life. But at the saddest and most difficult times of life there is only one set of footprints. This is not a sign of the Lord's absence when he is most needed, but that at those times he is carrying us in his arms. It is possible that the origins of this well-known poem are actually in the Bible. In the first chapter of the Book of Deuteronomy Moses speaks to the people of Israel about the search for the Promised Land and says 'the Lord God has continued to support you, as a man supports his son, all along the road you followed until you arrived here' (Deut. 1:31).

[3] Pope Benedict XVI, Angelus address, 14 March 2010.

- Can you think of times when you may have acted like the younger son, or the older son, or the father in the parable of the prodigal son?
- What is the most challenging aspect of the parable of the prodigal son?
- Can you think of difficult times in your journey of faith when you have sensed God's support?

I remember vividly when we had a phone installed at home in Derby. The bright red phone was on a table at the bottom of the stairs. I was sat on the bottom step with one of my brothers staring at this new-fangled contraption. What we did not know was that one of our elder brothers had gone to the top of the street and from the phone box dialed our number. The loud ring on the new phone made us jump: what do you do now?

'It's only me.' For some people this might be an opening line in telephone conversations, especially among an older, pre-text, pre-App generation. That phrase is a means of providing information. How times have changed. In the very opening scene of *The Two Popes*, the newly-installed Pope Francis is on the phone to Skytours to book a flight to Lampedusa and when he confirms he is 'Bergoglio' living in the Vatican City, just like the pope, the customer service operator responds, 'Very funny', and the line goes dead.

'I have called you by your name, you are mine' (Isa. 43:1). God looks out for us because God has called us by name, not for information, but to be part of a family. It is a call which accompanies us throughout the journey of life, even if we go astray. So it is never 'only me', for God called me first, by name, and accompanies me forever on the journey. There will be times when I feel lost, but someone is calling me by name. As a popular hymn states, 'When the fear of loneliness is looming, then remember I am at your side, Do not be afraid'.[4] God has called us to pursue a path, to set out on a journey along which we are called by name, not because God needs information, but because God loves us. It is as simple as that.

The journey of life, then, is not solitary, but nor is it the most direct of routes; it is full of twists and turns. Inevitably there will be times when we feel lost, or when everything appears to go wrong. A very human reaction would be to throw in the towel, to give up. One of the great challenges of faith is surely to accept that God does not throw in the towel, God does not give up. But more importantly, it is a reassurance that God's love for us never wavers. God has

[4] 'Do Not Be Afraid, For I Have Redeemed You', words by Gerard Markland, published by Kevin Mayhew Ltd, 1978.

called us by name and will continue to do so. In his homily about the lost sheep a fourth-century bishop, St Asterius of Amasea, notes that when the shepherd finally found the lost sheep he did not chase it back to the rest of the flock, shouting at it and beating it. He 'gently placed it on his own shoulders and carried it back to the flock'.[5] That is an act of tenderness and love, a welcome home. Such is God's welcome for us, whom God has called by name. No matter how difficult the journey, no matter how many mistakes are made, or how many times I lose my way, God 'will not give up'.

Prayer

Lord, you called me by name, you show me the path of life. When I feel lost, show me the light of your footsteps so that I may walk at your side, knowing that only you can guide me along the right path towards the bright light of heaven.

[5] An excerpt from Saint Asterius of Amasea's meditation on the Good Shepherd is used in the Roman Catholic Office of Readings for Thursday of the First Week in Lent.

Further reflection

Dear Young Friends,

I know that this evening you are keeping a vigil
of prayer, you are praying.

And I know that others are still on their way,
journeying here.

How beautiful these two things are: to pray
and to journey!

There are two things that we have to do in life.

We have to keep our hearts open to God,

since we receive our strength from him,

and we have to keep journeying,

because in life one can never stand still.

A young person cannot retire at the age of
twenty!

He or she must keep walking.

He or she must always keep moving forward,
always going uphill.

One of you can say to me:

'Yes, Father, but sometimes I am weak and I
fall'.

That doesn't make any difference!

There is an old Alpine song that says:

'In the art of climbing, the important thing is
not to keep from falling,

but never to remain down on the ground'.

I offer you these two pieces of advice.

THE JOURNEY

Never stay down, immediately get up;
let someone help you to get up.
That's the first thing. The second thing is:
Don't spend your life sitting on a couch!
Live your life, build your life, do it, keep moving
*   forward!*
Keep advancing on the journey,
get involved and you find extraordinary
*   happiness.*
I can assure you of that.

Pope Francis, 20 November 2019

Listening

Watch the discussion after supper in Castel
Gandolfo between Pope Benedict XVI and
Cardinal Bergoglio.

> (33 minutes into the film, a 5-minute scene)

'You know… the hardest thing is to listen, to
hear his voice, God's voice. When I was a young
man – hundreds of years ago – I always knew
what he wanted of me, what God wanted, what
purpose he had for me. But now, I don't know
– perhaps I need to listen more intently … I
think perhaps I need a spiritual hearing aid.
Who does know? You know when I first heard
that voice, whatever that was, his voice, God's
voice, it brought me peace. Such peace.'

Pope Benedict XVI

'Now keep quiet and listen, pay attention and
listen.' I can still remember such instructions from
my schoolteachers, and they probably had to say
it far too often! Of course, today the instruction is

more likely to be 'Switch off your phones!' I can also remember the times when we would go out to play with precise instructions from mum or dad about where to go, what time to be in, and so on. Some minor disaster would occur, such as losing the football or coming in slightly late, to be greeted with the words 'Now what did I tell you, where have you been, what time do you call this?'

In the 1990s, many train companies in the UK introduced Quiet Coaches. Mobile technology was in its infancy and telephone conversations could be loud and annoying. Many phone users seemed to think that because you were talking on a mobile phone you had to speak louder. I have heard people carefully, slowly and loudly giving out all their bank details; and even, sadly, ending a relationship via mobile phone in the middle of the Quiet Coach surrounded by fellow passengers who had become an unwilling audience in the tragic drama unfolding in Coach D. Ironically, many train companies began to scrap Quiet Coaches because they were causing too many rows among passengers. Staff were to ask people to be nice to each other instead. Not to be outdone, Italy's high-speed train *Frecciarossa* now has Business Quiet and Standard Silenzio areas in which no external sounds are permitted. Having lived in Rome for many years, it strikes me that Italians are not the quietest of people and they love their phones. Silence would be more unsettling than noise!

- How does the day begin: with stillness or an immediate check on the mobile phone?
- Is there any quiet time in your day or just the absence of noise?
- How do you or would you use a quiet time?

The sixth-century *Rule of Monasteries*, better known as the *Rule of St Benedict*, written in Latin, begins: '*Obsculta, o fili, praecepta magistri, et inclina aurem cordis tui*.' 'Listen carefully, my son, to the master's instructions, and attend to them with the ear of your heart.' At the end of the parable of the sower in Matthew's gospel Jesus says 'Anyone who has ears should listen!' (Matt 13:9), and in the Book of Revelation the voice speaking to John says, 'Let anyone who can hear, listen to what the Spirit is saying to the churches' (Rev. 2:29). In the Letter of James one reads 'You should know this, my dear brothers and sisters: everyone should be swift to listen but slow to speak and slow to anger' (Jas. 1:19).

Listening is important and especially when living in a world full of noise. Many of us may have had the annoying experience of being on a train or bus and being able to hear someone's music through their headphones, or, to be more precise, just hearing a monotonous, loud beat which constantly sounds the same! Then, of course, there is the dilemma of whether you have the courage to go up and ask the music-lover to turn the music down. Even the weekly or monthly shop in the supermarket is devoid of the sound of silence. Market research suggests that music playing in the background as you stroll gently down the aisle (no, not that aisle!) has a calming influence and encourages the shopper to spend more time browsing and therefore spending. Everywhere, the sound of noise.

At the transfiguration of Jesus recounted in the gospel of Mark, God's voice from heaven says, 'This is my Son, the beloved. Listen to him' (Mark 9:7). This suggests that the true relationship with the Lord is rooted in listening. To learn to listen requires an ability to appreciate silence, even to create silence, for it can only be in silence that we learn to listen. Spiritual retreats can often be a time for creating space for silence. My abiding memory of one of the first 'silent' retreats in which I participated is of a fellow retreatant sitting opposite me at breakfast slowly falling asleep. For once, I can safely say it was not my less-than-enlightening social chit-chat that sent someone to sleep! The season of Lent can often provide such an opportunity to get away from the hustle-and-bustle of everyday life, spend some time in silence, and review the spiritual life. 'Lent is supposed to be a time when we review our spiritual life, think again about what it means to be a follower of Christ, reset the compass of our discipleship and prepare ourselves to celebrate the Easter festival. But often we just give up biscuits.'[6] On Ash Wednesday 2020, Pope Francis said that Lent was a time 'to turn off the television ... to tear ourselves away from our mobile phone and connect ourselves to the Gospel. It's the time,' the pope said, 'to give up useless words, slander, rumours and gossip, and to speak and give oneself to the Lord.'

In a 2018 documentary film *Pope Francis: A Man of His Word*, Pope Francis talks about St Francis as a revitalisation of the figure of Christ, a man of patience, understanding and dialogue. 'He was the apostle of the ear,' the pope said, 'knowing how to listen.' He continued:

At times, the speed of the modern world, its frenzy, keeps us from listening well to what others are saying. Someone is halfway through a dialogue, and we already interrupt and want to answer before the other one has finished

[6]   Stephen Cottrell, *I Thirst: The Cross – The Great Triumph of Love* (London, Hodder & Stoughton, 2019), p. 12.

talking. Not losing the capacity to listen? And Francis is a listener. He listened to the voice of God, he listened to the voice of the poor, to the voice of the sick, and to the voice of nature. And he transformed all of this into a way of life. And I hope that the seed of Francis grows in many hearts.

- There is a popular proverb 'God gave us two ears and one mouth to be used in those proportions.' What do you think this means?
- What do you think 'to listen' really means? Is it easy to listen to someone else?
- What does 'apostle of the ear' mean and what skills might be required?

In *The Two Popes*, Pope Benedict XVI acknowledges that 'the hardest thing is to listen, to hear his voice'. The two parts of this phrase are distinct, but connected, and probably common to all of us. In our frenetic, busy world have we lost the ability to listen, to be 'apostles of the ear'? The art of listening requires silence on the part of the listener and silence today may be such a rarity that perhaps we have become fearful of silence. Many churches have signs or a notice in the service sheet or newsletter rightly reminding worshippers that the church is a place of stillness and quiet, a place of prayer, and yet in a number of churches noise levels seem to increase dramatically as the start of the religious service draws closer. Of course, it may be the sound of increasingly fervent prayer rising towards heaven and not the exchange of social chit-chat. While I know space can often be at a premium, it is interesting that in some churches tea and coffee is immediately available in the place where moments previously worshippers were being encouraged to participate in silent worship – that challenging distinction about the boundaries between social and sacred space. I remember a priest who worked in the Vatican for more than 40 years and used to walk past St Peter's Basilica every day on his way to work, but never set foot inside the Basilica for many, many years. 'It's not a church anymore,' he used to say, 'it's just a tourist attraction.'

It is hard to listen and that might be because it is hard to be silent. Pope Francis once said, 'If we go to pray, for example, before the Crucifix, and we talk, talk, talk, and then we leave, we do not listen to Jesus. We do not allow him to speak to our heart. Listen: this is the key word. Do not forget!'[7]

'The root of peace lies in the capacity to listen,' Pope Francis said in July 2017. In The Two Popes, Pope Benedict XVI recalls how clearly he used to

[7]   Pope Francis, Angelus address, 17 July 2016.

hear the voice of God, and it 'brought me peace. Such peace'. And in a wonderful phrase with which many of us can resonate, he says that perhaps he now needs 'a spiritual hearing aid'.

Hearing, discerning the voice of God, is one of the biggest challenges in the spiritual life, on the journey of faith. Jesus himself taught us to pray, giving us the prayer we recite today as the Our Father, the Lord's Prayer. One of its simple petitions is: 'Your will be done on earth, as it is in heaven.' Many years ago I asked a wise spiritual director if God always answers prayer. 'Yes', was the comforting reply. 'But sometimes the answer might be "No"', he added. The Our Father asks that God's will be done, it does not say, 'Your will be done on earth as long as it fits in with mine.'

In *The Two Popes* it seems Pope Benedict XVI may be having one of those arid, desert experiences about which many spiritual fathers have written down the centuries, a period of spiritual desolation expressed in the poem *Dark Night of the Soul* written by the sixteenth-century Spanish mystic St John of the Cross. Where is the voice of God? Why has God gone silent? Is God there at all? 'I pray ... but only silence,' are the words put on the lips of Pope Benedict XVI. I suspect many of us could echo those words, a result of that frustrating experience of thinking we are praying just as we were taught, using all the right words and techniques, to be greeted by what we think is just empty, desolate silence.

It is easy to recite the traditional definition of prayer as the raising of the mind and heart to God. But prayer can seem like a one-way street, an empty endeavour that does not nourish daily life, does not sustain me or assist me in facing the challenges of the modern world. The mind and heart are raised, but silence. Why do I bother? In such circumstances, prayer can be discouraging; the desert experience expressed by Pope Benedict in the film can be something all-too-real and not a mirage at all. Has God completely abandoned me? Is it time to put on the spiritual hearing aid?

The late Cardinal Basil Hume, Archbishop of Westminster from 1976-1999, used the simple imagery of a staircase to teach us something about prayer:

> I think of a small child learning to walk, and the father is at the top of the stairs. The child is not yet old enough, indeed is too weak to climb those stairs on his own. Every time he puts his foot on the first step he falls over backwards. He tries it several times with unfortunate and unsuccessful results. The father is standing at the top of the stairs watching. Now, the child

has a number of options. He can sit down at the bottom of the stairs and howl with frustration and fury (when did I last howl with frustration and fury?) because he can't do it. Or he can take another option and say this is no good and push off into another room. So it is either getting angry or giving up. But the father wants to see the child go on trying to get up the stairs. It's obvious what must happen. Since the child is too weak, but showing willing, the father goes down the stairs, picks up the child and carries him to the top. That is the way it is. Our part is to go on trying, putting our foot on that first step, painfully, doggedly. Then from time to time the Father will come down, pick us up and carry us to the top. In God's way of doing things, if He ever does carry us to the top, He then always puts us back again at the bottom of the stairs to start all over again. It is only right at the end of life that He takes us to the top and keeps us there.[8]

- Where do you find silence in daily life? Does silence belong in church and are our churches places of silence and prayer?
- Are there times when you think God has not

[8] Basil Hume OSB, *To Be A Pilgrim* (Slough, St Paul Publications, 1984), p. 138.

heard you, that God is absent, that you have experienced that dark night of the soul?

• Have there been times when you have sensed God speaking not through prayer but through places, people and events?

The ability to listen, to spend time regularly in prayer is the bedrock of the journey of faith. In the first week of Lent each year, the pope and the Vatican curia go on retreat away from the Vatican, a week-long opportunity to re-charge the spiritual batteries. It is an opportunity to listen without the distractions of day-to-day business. Such a retreat into the desert is a journey into a life-giving desert, not the dry, arid place of death, as Pope Francis explained to pilgrims just before the start of Lent 2020:

> Behold the desert, place of life not of death, because to converse with the Lord in silence restores life to us ... The desert is the place of the essential. Let us look at our lives: how many useless things surround us! We pursue a thousand things that seem necessary and in reality, aren't so. How much good it would do us to be free of so many superfluous realities, to rediscover what counts, to rediscover the face of the One next to us! On this also Jesus

gives us the example by fasting. To fast is not only to slim down, to fast is in fact to go to the essential and to seek the beauty of a simpler life.[9]

But prayer is not easy, even for popes. A simple, human statement of fact by Pope Francis in 2017 led to amazing headlines even in such august media outlets as the BBC and some of the national broadsheets in the UK: 'Pope admits he sometimes falls asleep while praying.' The detail contained in some of the news reports still makes me smile: the pope 'often prays for long periods with his eyes closed', and 'Vatican sources' said that the pope's hectic schedule was only possible 'because he gets his head down for a snooze after lunch'. It must have been a quiet news day if someone falling asleep while praying and regularly taking a siesta was headline news.

On his official Twitter account, Pope Francis has written: 'If you find it hard to pray, don't give up. Be still; make space for God to come in; let Him look at you, and He will fill you with His peace.'[10] Prayer *is* difficult, listening *is* difficult, but it is important not to give up. Of course, what adds to

[9] Pope Francis, General Audience, 26 February 2020.
[10] Pope Francis, official Twitter page (@Pontifex), 26 March 2020.

the difficulty is the nature of today's society where instant answers are demanded all the time. The oft-quoted saying 'Patience is a virtue' must apply to prayer, too. It is interesting that Pope Francis suggests above that we must 'make space for God to come in'. The sixteenth-century Spanish mystic St Teresa of Avila asked: 'Why do you look for God here, why do you look there? God is within you.'

In *The Two Popes* Benedict XVI indicated the need for a spiritual hearing aid. St Teresa of Avila emphasises the need to look in the right place, too, if we are to listen to God, to hear God's voice in the midst of the cacophony of today's world. An Arab proverb states that 'Prayer is the pillow of religion'. All the indications are that without listening to God, without prayer, our lives might run the risk of not being so much a search for the Other, or Another, but a daily routine focused on Me, a journey of self-desire and self-gratification.

In a touching scene in the film shortly before he announces his intention to relinquish the papal office, Pope Benedict XVI says that he does now hear the voice of the Lord; 'and the voice is the last one I expected to hear him speak with, it is your voice', he says to Cardinal Bergoglio. 'I think,' he continues, 'perhaps I could not hear him not because he was withdrawing from me, but because he was saying, "Go, my faithful servant".'

The challenge of listening to God is not only that you might not get the answer you were expecting, but it might come from unexpected quarters, too. This calls to mind the words of the Jesuit poet Gerard Manley Hopkins (1844-1889):

> for Christ plays in ten thousand places
> Lovely in limbs, and lovely in eyes not his
> To the Father through the features of men's
> faces.[11]

'And look, I am with you always till the end of time' (Matt. 28:20); 'Be still and know I am God' (Ps. 46:10); 'Speak, Lord; for your servant is listening' (1 Sam. 3:10). Sometimes, prayer is just about listening, being present. As God has promised, God is there. He will respond, too, but sometimes that response may not come in prayer. God may speak through things that happen, through the people we meet, through the opportunities presented to us each day. On Mount Horeb, Elijah finds God not in the mighty wind, or the earthquake, or the fire: 'And after the fire there was a light sound of silence. And when Elijah heard this, he covered his face with his cloak and went out and stood at the entrance of the cave' (1 Kings 19:12-13). God was to be found where Elijah least expected.

[11]   Gerard Manley Hopkins, *As Kingfishers Catch Fire*.

Prayer

Lord, your servant is trying to learn how to recognise your voice however and wherever you speak. Speak, Lord, your servant is listening.

Further reflection

> *Dear brothers and sisters, let us learn to*
> *pause longer before God,*
> *who revealed himself in Jesus Christ,*
> *let us learn to recognise in silence, in our own*
> *hearts,*
> *his voice that calls us and leads us back to*
> *the depths of our existence,*
> *to the source of life, to the source of*
> *salvation,*
> *to enable us to go beyond the limitations of*
> *our life and*
> *to open ourselves to God's dimension,*
> *to the relationship with him, which is Infinite*
> *Love.*

Pope Benedict XVI, 11 May 2011

Change

Watch Pope Benedict XVI and Cardinal Bergoglio continuing their discussion at the tea table in the garden at Castel Gandolfo.

(26 minutes into the film, a 6-minute scene)

'I changed' (F) n(B) ?
'No. You compromised' (B)
'No. I changed. It's a different thing. Life – the life he gave us – is all change'
'God does not change!'
'Yes. He does. He moves towards us as we ...'
'I am the way! The truth! And the life! Where should we find him if he is always moving?'
'On the journey?'

'I wish you'd just grow up.' I wonder how many times we have been told that or used those words ourselves. Addressed to a child or a young person, it implies their ideas or behaviour are childish or juvenile. There is also perhaps a suggestion from the speaker that he or she is addressing the listener from a perspective of perceived wisdom, that all will be well when the child or young person has achieved an appropriate level of maturity and wisdom – implicitly that of the speaker. In other words, once they have changed. Growing up means we see things with the eyes of a child, then perhaps through the eyes of a rebellious teenager, and so on. Change is part of life.

Brian Clough (1935-2004) was a forthright, outspoken football manager. In a TV interview he was once asked what he would do if a member of his playing staff thought the way Clough was doing things was wrong. 'Well,' Clough replied, 'I'd ask him which way he thinks it should be done, we get down to it, we talk about it for 20 minutes and then we decide I was right.' No change, and certainly no compromise, in that situation. But change is an inevitable part of life. Writing to the people of Corinth in AD 53-57, St Paul states quite clearly: 'When I was a child, I spoke as a child, I thought as a child, I reasoned as a child. When I became a man, I put aside the things of childhood' (1 Cor. 13:11).

The idea of change, the challenge of change, regularly occurs in *The Two Popes*. After the first unsuccessful scrutiny while the cardinals are eating together, Cardinal Hummes refers to the number of votes already garnered for 'real change', while Cardinal Ratzinger himself talks to other cardinal-electors about the need for 'one common reference point, one unchanging eternal truth'. When Pope Benedict XVI and Cardinal Bergoglio are chatting in the Vatican gardens, the old adage crops up in conversation: 'A church that marries the spirit of the age will be widowed in the next.' The discussion turns on whether Bergoglio, once the very traditional leader of the Jesuits in Argentina, but now portrayed as a liberal, outspoken archbishop, has changed or compromised. By extension, does God change or does God evolve and move towards us, as Cardinal Bergoglio suggests.

In his First Letter to the people of Corinth cited earlier, St Paul seems to be indicating that it is our relationship with God which changes, matures over time. For some people one of their earliest understandings of God may have been of an old man with a long, white beard, probably sitting on a cloud. The discussion in *The Two Popes* is not about a particular portrayal of the divine, but about the impact of faith and belief on daily life. The world in which we live and express our belief is ever-changing, is probably already very different even from the world of our own childhood. Furthermore, it is an increasingly secular world where there can be pressure to limit faith to the private sphere. There is a scene in the drama television series *The New Pope* where Pope John Paul III receives in audience the actress Sharon Stone, playing herself. She asks the pope to change Church teaching on same-sex marriage. 'Can't the Bible be upgraded?', she asks. In reply Pope John Paul III notes that, 'Alas, the Bible is not an iPhone. Anything that can be upgraded, like an iPhone, eventually ends up in the bin, only to be replaced by a more expensive model. The Bible has endured for a very long time, and its value has changed a little, if at all.'

- Can you recall times when you have been told to 'grow up' or when you have told others to do so?
- What sort of things do you look at so differently now because of the maturity brought by experience and the wisdom of years?
- Are there some matters of faith or Church teaching that you also look at differently, or even might like to see 'upgraded'? If so, why?

Calling to mind how often each of us may have been told to grow up or citing a football manager who was famous more than thirty years ago pale into absolute insignificance when we think of the way our lives have been changed by the coronavirus pandemic and the spread of COVID-19. Addressing the Irish nation on St Patrick's Day, the Taoiseach Leo Varadkar said it was a St Patrick's Day '... like no other. A day that none of us will forget. Today's children will tell their own children and grandchildren about the national holiday in 2020 that had no parades or parties, but instead saw everyone staying at home to protect each other.' And he added the stirring phrase: 'In years to come, let them say of us, when things were at their worst, we were at our best.'

The next day the Catholic Bishops of England and Wales said there were to be no public acts of worship until further notice and the celebration of Mass was to take place without a public congregation. 'Knowing that the Mass is being celebrated; joining in spiritually in that celebration; watching the live-streaming of Mass; following its prayers at home; making an act of spiritual communion: this is how we share in the Sacrifice of Christ in these days. These are the ways in which we will sanctify Sunday, and indeed every day.'[12]

A pope and a Church that wants its priests

[12] A letter from the President and Vice-President on behalf of all the Bishops of the Conference, 18 March 2020.

and bishops to have the 'smell of the sheep'[13] has had to learn, like the rest of society, the language of social distancing and self-isolation. A Church which sets great store by the importance, indeed the obligation, to attend Sunday Mass, had to remove that obligation. I remember many years ago in Canon Law lectures questions being posed about how late one can arrive for Mass for your attendance still to be valid – a far cry from the live-streaming, digital church, with celebrations in the absence of a public congregation.

An article in a national newspaper said that one of the most frightening things about the Coronavirus situation was:

> its exposure of how fragile our way of life is. We might have felt that our 'civilised life' was unassailable, that the events, rituals and institutions which anchor our lives were set in concrete, but no: public services creak, elections are postponed, families are separated, culture is cancelled, sport is on hold, churches, mosques and synagogues close. When the rug of normality is pulled

---

[13] 'This I ask of you: be shepherds, with the "smell of the sheep," make it real, as shepherds among your flock, fishers of men,' Homily of Pope Francis, Chrism Mass, Saint Peter's Basilica, 28 March 2013.

from under us like this, the inevitable result is anxiety. We are unanchored, unsure of what will happen next.[14]

In *The Two Popes*, Benedict XVI says that God, the Way, the Truth and the Life, the anchor of life itself, does not change. Bergoglio, on the other hand, suggests that nothing is static, not even God, he is moving towards us. God, the Way, the Truth, and the Life, can be found on the glorious journey of life.

Perhaps both are right. God does not change. He is not that old man with a white beard sitting on a cloud. The God of Scripture is love, truth, justice and light, merciful and forgiving. This is the God who created us, who accompanies us on the journey, the unchanging God. 'Jesus Christ is the same today as he was yesterday and as he will be for ever' (Heb. 13:8). But God does not simply sit still and wait for us to seek God out. Like the father of the prodigal son God is looking out for us, like the Good Shepherd, actively seeking out the lost, to set them again on the right path.

So if God is unchanging, what about faith, Church teaching, how faith is lived out and expressed each day? For example, some people

[14]   'Anxiety is viral but we don't have to catch it,' Clare Foges, *The Times*, 16 March 2020, p. 25.

think that the teaching of the Catholic Church never changes, citing the old adage 'Rome has spoken, the case is closed.' Of course, this is not so, for change is part of history. But change can always make us uneasy. On 25 January 1959, Pope John XXIII announced to a small group of cardinals his intention to summon a general council of the Church, a monumental event which became known as the Second Vatican Council. Perhaps sensing that unwelcome change was in the offing, it is said that some of the traditional cardinals of the Roman curia tried to dissuade the pope. 'It will be absolutely impossible to prepare such an event for 1963,' one said. 'Fine,' Pope John XXIII is alleged to have replied, 'we'll open it in 1962.' And so he did on 11 October 1962.

- Do you find change challenging or frightening?
- How has the coronavirus pandemic changed your community and your life of faith?
- 'This church building is closed. The Church is out there.' Can you think of ways in which community life and the life of faith have been mutually enriched in the physical absence of church?

'To live is to change, and to be perfect is to have changed often,' wrote Saint Cardinal John

Henry Newman (1801-1890) in his *Essay on the Development of Christian Doctrine* (1845). In the book *Salt of the Earth*, Pope Benedict XVI was asked about the view that there were two Ratzingers, one before Rome, a progressive, and then the orthodox guardian of the faith later working in Rome. He replied:

> I think I have already made the essential point that the basic decision of my life is continuous, that I believe in God, in Christ, in the Church, and try to orient my life accordingly ... I don't deny there has been development and change within a fundamental identity and that I, precisely in changing, have tried to remain faithful to what I have always had at heart. Here I agree with Cardinal Newman, who says that to live is to change and that the one who was capable of changing has lived much.[15]

The challenge of being a Christian in today's society is about being truthful to and maintaining that fundamental Christian identity; about ensuring that the basic faith decision of our lives is continuous. In *The Two Popes*, Bergoglio declares that he no longer wishes to be a salesman for a

[15]   Joseph Cardinal Ratzinger, *Salt of the Earth* (San Francisco, Ignatius Press, 1997), p. 116.

product 'that I cannot in all conscience endorse'. In going from a conservative Jesuit provincial to a progressive archbishop he claims he has changed; Ratzinger believes he has compromised. How ironic, perhaps, that in a later discussion in the Sistine Chapel, Pope Benedict acknowledges that one of the reasons he did not want to resign was in case Bergoglio were elected – but now he, Pope Benedict, has changed. 'You compromised,' replies Bergoglio. 'No. I've changed. It's a different thing,' Pope Benedict confidently declares.

The temptation is there for each one of us to adopt an à-la-carte view of faith, to pick and choose the bits we believe, or the bits in which it is most convenient to believe and forget the rest. Is this being true to our identity as Christians or is it creating, adopting an identity more suitable to the whims of modern society? God is unchanging; to live is to change, to witness to our faith in the midst of the unprecedented challenges of modern-day society, instead of jettisoning everything, is the real challenge.

Saint Pope John XXIII wrote: 'We are not on earth as museum-keepers, but to cultivate a flourishing garden of life and to prepare a glorious future.'[16] This is the same pope who, on

---

[16] Cited in Peter Hebblethwaite, *John XXIII Pope of the Council* (London, Geoffrey Chapman, 1984) p. 269.

summoning the Second Vatican Council, wrote about the need for the Catholic Church 'to read the signs of the times' and proclaim the Gospel in the rapidly changing circumstances of the modern world. Although written nearly sixty years ago, the pope's words reverberate so powerfully in today's challenging circumstances:

> Today the Church is witnessing a crisis underway within society. While humanity is at the threshold of a new age, immensely serious and broad tasks await the Church, as in the most tragic periods of her history. It is a question in fact of bringing the perennial life-giving energies of the Gospel to the modern world, a world that boasts of its technical and scientific conquests but also bears the effects of a temporal order that some have wanted to reorganise by excluding God.[17]

And it was this same pope who on his death-bed said, 'It is not that the Gospel has changed: it is that we have begun to understand it better ... the moment has come to discern the signs of the times,

[17]   John XXIII, Apostolic Constitution *Humanae salutis*, 25 December 1961. The official Latin text may be found in AAS 54 (1962) 5-13.

to seize the opportunity and to look far ahead.'[18] Pope Francis, too, preaching in the chapel in the Domus Sanctae Marthae on 23 October 2015 said, 'Times change and we Christians must constantly change. We must change, steadfast in the faith in Jesus Christ, steadfast in the truth of the Gospel, but our approach must constantly move according to the signs of the time.'

Faith is not about keeping pristine and safe from harm the contents of a museum. It is about witnessing to the faith in a world so much in need of witnesses of the Gospel. In very general terms the dilemma perhaps implied in *The Two Popes*, the issue played out in front of the viewer, is about whether the modern-day believer should adapt to the signs, even the pressures, of the times, or remain steadfast with an unchanging view of faith.

Three short verses in Matthew's gospel provide a good starting-point to explore the idea of change and steadfastness:

Therefore, everyone who hears these words of mine and acts on them will be like a sensible person who built a house on rock. Rain came down, floods rose, gales blew and hurled themselves against that house, and it did not

18   Peter Hebblethwaite, *op. cit.,* p. 499.

fall: it was founded on rock. But everyone who hears these words of mine and does not act on them will be like a stupid person who built a house on sand. Rain came down, floods rose, gales blew and struck that house, and it fell; and what a fall it had! (Matt. 7:24-27)

Jesus invites us to build our faith not on the blowing sands of time, but on the rock which is the living encounter with God. Of course, that does not mean to say a life of faith will always be easy, even less that we will have all the answers. Things around us may change, but Jesus is inviting us to make God the one thing that does not change in our lives, to place our trust in God. He is, as Benedict XVI says in the film, the Way, the Truth, and the Life.

But what if we place our trust in, and root our lives in God, and then find ourselves in a world in which the rug of normalcy has disappeared, and, to many, it seems very clear that either God does not exist or is just not bothered anymore. At such a time of trial, isn't it tempting just to change tack and throw in the towel?

- Have there been times when you have wanted to throw in the towel, when believing has just been too much?
- Or are there any elements of our faith and

worship which provide security and comfort in times of trouble?

- What are the constant, fundamental elements of your faith?

At the height of the coronavirus pandemic in Italy, Pope Francis led a special prayer service in a deserted but rain-swept St Peter's Square. He preached on the gospel passage in Mark where Jesus, asleep in the stern of the boat, eventually calms the storm (Mark 4:35-41). The pope's words are a profound reflection on the call for change and trust which is addressed to us each day of our lives:

'Why are you afraid? Have you no faith?' Lord, you are calling to us, calling us to faith. Which is not so much believing that you exist, but coming to you and trusting in you. This Lent your call reverberates urgently: 'Be converted!', 'Return to me with all your heart' (Joel 2:12). You are calling on us to seize this time of trial as a *time of choosing*. It is not the time of your judgement, but of our judgement: a time to choose what matters and what passes away, a time to separate what is necessary from what is not. It is a time to get our lives back on track with regard to you, Lord, and to others. We

can look to so many exemplary companions for the journey, who, even though fearful, have reacted by giving their lives. This is the force of the Spirit poured out and fashioned in courageous and generous self-denial. It is the life in the Spirit that can redeem, value and demonstrate how our lives are woven together and sustained by ordinary people – often forgotten people – who do not appear in newspaper and magazine headlines nor on the grand catwalks of the latest show, but who without any doubt are in these very days writing the decisive events of our time.[19]

Choosing what is important often leads to change. A parish priest once told me how easy it is for all of us to have a firm grasp of the non-essentials. In the dialogue between Bergoglio and Pope Benedict about change and compromise, the former acknowledges that in the past he was very conservative in his outlook, he made seminarians wear cassocks all day, even when working in the vegetable garden. But he has now changed and, perhaps to paraphrase Pope Saint John XXIII, is trying to discern the signs of the times and find the

[19] Extraordinary Moment of Prayer presided over by Pope Francis, Sagrato of St Peter's Basilica, 27 March 2020.

God he believes in moving towards us. However, as we have noted, Pope Benedict seems to suggest God is unchanging. The scene in the garden ends with a wonderful exchange which speaks so eloquently to our challenging lives today, as Pope Benedict asks 'Where should we find him if he is always moving?' 'On the journey?' Bergoglio tentatively suggests. As they move into an unfamiliar part of the garden, Bergoglio suggests they find some shade. 'Yes,' says Pope Benedict, 'and perhaps we'll find God over there. On "the journey"! I'll introduce you to him.'

In the storm-tossed boat journeying across the lake the disciples realised that Jesus does care for them, does look out for them, and provides the rootedness of faith. For us, circumstances will change, we are called to proclaim the Gospel in very different circumstances every day of our lives, but our hope is rooted in what does not change: 'Like the disciples, we will experience that with [Jesus] on board there will be no shipwreck. Because this is God's strength: turning to the good everything that happens to us, even the bad things. He brings serenity into our storms, because with God life never dies.'[20]

And still we might say: 'But what is the point? God might transform the good that happens to

[20]   *Ibid.*

us, but I still do not understand, still feel lost and weak in the sea of change.' In *The Two Popes*, Bergoglio provides the spiritual answer: 'It is our weakness that calls forth the grace of God. You show your weakness, he gives us strength' – the unchanging God espoused by Benedict XVI in an earlier dialogue. Another response to that uncertainty is provided again by Saint Cardinal John Henry Newman, in a well-known passage from his *Meditations on Christian Doctrine* quoted by Pope Benedict XVI during his visit to the United Kingdom for the beatification of Cardinal Newman in September 2010. The pope was talking about the Christian who serves the one true Master, not the whims and changing tides of the world, and in so doing is guided by the principles of faith. Newman helps us understand what this means for our daily lives:

God has created me to do Him some definite service. He has committed some work to me which He has not committed to another. I have my mission. I may never know it in this life, but I shall be told it in the next. I am a link in a chain, a bond of connection between persons. He has not created me for naught. I shall do good; I shall do His work. I shall be an angel of peace, a preacher of truth in my own place, while not intending it if I do but keep His commandments. Therefore, I will trust Him, whatever I am, I can never be thrown away. If I am in sickness, my sickness may serve Him, in perplexity, my perplexity may serve Him. If I am in sorrow, my sorrow may serve Him. He does nothing in vain. He knows what He is about. He may take away my friends. He may throw me among strangers. He may make me feel desolate, make my spirits sink, hide my future from me. Still, He knows what He is about.[21]

Prayer

Lord, in these challenging times and storm-tossed seas may I feel your comforting presence. Give me the strength which comes from a faith built on the rock which is Christ my Lord. With an identity rooted in you, may I proclaim the Gospel to build the communities which will shape the world of tomorrow.

[21] John Henry Newman, *Meditations and Devotions*, 'Mediations on Christian Doctrine', 'Hope in God-Creator', 7 March 1848, 301-2.

Further reflection

What we are experiencing is not simply an
epoch of changes,
but an epochal change.
*We find ourselves living at a time when
change*
is no longer linear, but epochal.
*It entails decisions that rapidly transform our
ways of living,*
*of relating to one another, of communicating
and thinking,*
*of how different generations relate to one
another*
*and how we understand and experience faith
and science.*
*Often we approach change as if it were a
matter of simply putting on new clothes,*
but remaining exactly as we were before.
*I think of the enigmatic expression found in a
famous Italian novel:*
*'If we want everything to stay the same, then
everything has to change'.*
*Cardinal Martini, in his last interview, a few
days before his death,*
said something that should make us think:
*'The Church is two hundred years behind the
times.*

THE GLORIOUS JOURNEY

Why is she not shaken up? Are we afraid?
    Fear, instead of courage?
Yet faith is the Church's foundation.
Faith, confidence, courage ... Only
    love conquers weariness'.
... Divine love ... inspires, guides and corrects
    change,
and overcomes the human fear of leaving
    behind 'security'
in order once more to embrace the 'mystery'.

Pope Francis, 21 December 2019

Mercy

Watch Cardinal Bergoglio's arrival in Rome and then in Castel Gandolfo, where he meets Pope Benedict XVI in the garden and they begin their conversation.

(19 minutes into the film, a 7-minute scene)

> 'Did Jesus build walls? His face is the face of mercy. The bigger the sinner, the warmer the welcome. Mercy is the dynamite that blows down walls.'
>
> **Cardinal Bergoglio**

As a young child I was taken to church every fortnight to confess my sins. 'Bless me, Father, for I have sinned. It is two weeks since my last confession and I have sworn, told lies, and taken God's name in vain.' My eight-year-old brain soon thought that the priest might recognise me from this fortnightly list of heinous crimes, and so to make identification absolutely impossible I would change the order in which I recited this shameful list: 'I have taken God's name in vain, sworn and told lies.' Still concerned that this wretched sinner would be identified and denied mercy and forgiveness, I decided to consult a battered old prayer book which had an 'Examination of Conscience.' Now, with my new-found knowledge I was sure I would definitely remain an anonymous sinner: 'It is two weeks since my last confession. Telling lies, taking God's name in vain, swearing, and arson.' I didn't even know the meaning of the word and nor had I done such a thing, I hasten to add! But it was close to the top of the list in the prayer book, so it must have been something serious and worthy of forgiveness. Clearly, I had no understanding of sin or, more importantly, God's mercy and forgiveness.

In religious usage there are two aspects to mercy, the divine and the human. In *The Two Popes*, Cardinal Bergoglio is talking about divine mercy as expressed in the divinity's attitude to humanity: '[Jesus'] face is mercy. The bigger the sinner, the warmer the welcome. Mercy is the dynamite that blows down walls.' The human aspect, on the other hand, is the basic moral duty which should characterise all human dealings, the mercy shown to others.

One of the great documents of Saint John Paul II, published in 1980, is entitled *Dives in*

Misericordia, the Latin text of the opening words: 'It is "God, who is rich in mercy" whom Jesus Christ has revealed to us as Father.'[22] The pope stated:

> The present-day mentality, more perhaps than that of people in the past, seems opposed to a God of mercy, and in fact tends to exclude from life and to remove from the human heart the very idea of mercy. The word and the concept of 'mercy' seem to cause uneasiness in man, who, thanks to the enormous development of science and technology, never before known in history, has become the master of the earth and has subdued and dominated it. This dominion over the earth, sometimes understood in a one-sided and superficial way, seems to have no room for mercy.[23]

The idea of mercy and forgiveness are central to one of the most dramatic days of Saint Pope John Paul II's long papacy. On 13 May 1981 in St Peter's Square Pope John Paul II was shot and wounded by a Turkish gunman, Mehmet Ali Ağca. The pope believed that his life had been saved thanks to the intervention by Our Lady of Fatima, whose feast day is 13 May. Visiting the shrine of Fatima three years

[22] Saint John Paul II, *Dives in Misericordia*, 1980, n. 1.
[23] Ibid., n. 2.

later, the pope donated to the shrine the bullet that had lodged in his body, and the bullet was later set in a crown of precious stones placed on the statue of Our Lady of Fatima. A marble plaque set in the cobblestones of St Peter's Square marks the exact spot where the attempted assassination took place. Speaking from his hospital bed a few days after the attempt, the pope said, 'I pray for the brother who wounded me, and whom I have sincerely forgiven.' Just over six months later, Pope John Paul II visited Mehmet in prison and held the hand that had held the gun that was meant to kill him. Alone they spoke for just over 20 minutes. 'What we talked about,' the pope said later, 'will have to remain a secret between him and me, I spoke to him as a brother whom I have pardoned, and who has my complete trust.'

- Is reciting a laundry list of sins really a true confession and expression of desire for mercy?
- Have you ever experienced a real sense of mercy and being forgiven, by God or by someone else?
- 'We all need to be forgiven by others, so we must all be ready to forgive' (Saint John Paul II). How difficult is that?

Fake Pope[24] is the title of a book published in Italian in 2018 looking at the fake news disseminated about Pope Francis since his election in 2013. Inevitably, a few pages are devoted to what the authors call the phrase which has become the 'symbol of the pontificate': 'Who am I to judge?' The authors point out that depending on the perspective of the reader, this phrase was either a further condemnation of Pope Francis or yet another sign of his great standing in the modern world.

On the return flight from Rio de Janeiro where he had celebrated World Youth Day in July 2013, the pope was asked about his intentions to confront an alleged gay lobby in the Vatican. Subsequent media reports focused on the now famous five words 'Who am I to judge?', but it is worth looking in detail at what Pope Francis said in the early part of his answer to that question:

> But if a person, whether it be a lay person, a priest or a religious sister, commits a sin and then converts, the Lord forgives, and when the Lord forgives, the Lord forgets and this is very important for our lives. When we confess our sins and we truly say, 'I have sinned in this',

[24] Nello Scavo and Roberto Beretta, *Fake Pope* (Cinisello Balsamo, Edizioni San Paolo, 2018).

the Lord forgets, and so we have no right not to forget, because otherwise we would run the risk of the Lord not forgetting our sins. That is a danger. This is important: a theology of sin. Many times I think of Saint Peter. He committed one of the worst sins, that is he denied Christ, and even with this sin they made him Pope. We have to think a great deal about that.

On the same flight, the pope was also asked about the reception of sacraments in the Catholic Church for the divorced and remarried. Here, too, his response focused on mercy:

This is an issue which frequently comes up. Mercy is something much larger than the one case you raised. I believe that this is the season of mercy. This new era we have entered, and the many problems in the Church – like the poor witness given by some priests, problems of corruption in the Church, the problem of clericalism for example – have left so many people hurt, left so much hurt. The Church is a mother: she has to go out to heal those who are hurting, with mercy. If the Lord never tires of forgiving, we have no other choice than this: first of all, to care for those who are hurting. The Church is a mother, and she must travel this path of mercy. And find a form of mercy for all. When the prodigal son returned home, I don't think his father told him: 'You, sit down and listen: what did you do with the money?' No! He celebrated! Then, perhaps, when the son was ready to speak, he spoke. The Church has to do this, when there is someone ... not only wait for them, but go out and find them! That is what mercy is.

Some of the very points made here by Pope Francis are echoed in *The Two Popes*. In a flashback scene in which Argentinian soldiers arrest two Jesuit priests who had been working on the missions, and who had in advance been ordered by Bergoglio to close their mission, the voice-over of Bergoglio talking to Benedict XVI states: 'It is not easy to entrust oneself to God's mercy. I know, he has a very special capacity for forgetting our mistakes. God forgets, but I don't.' Was Bergoglio complicit in the arrest of his two Jesuit colleagues, protecting the good name of the religious Order above the well-being of his priests?

As Bergoglio continues to reminisce, the viewer is shown priests and religious being shot, bodies thrown on railway lines, or thrown into the sea, still alive, from military planes. 'Many priests were seen as supporters of the armed resistance,'

Bergoglio tells Benedict XVI. The two priests in the Jesuit mission were arrested and tortured for months. One forgave him, and in *The Two Popes* we see them celebrating Mass together; the other died still believing he had been betrayed by his superior. 'This is not a time I am proud of', Bergoglio says.

Benedict XVI takes Bergoglio's account of the past as a confession of sins and tells him, 'Believe in the mercy that you preach.' The prayer that Jesus taught us is very clear: 'forgive us our debts as we have forgiven our debtors' (Matt 6:12); and, as if to reinforce the point, the passage in Matthew's gospel concludes: 'For if you forgive others their failings, your heavenly Father will forgive you yours; but if you do not forgive others, your Father will not forgive your failings either' (Matt. 6:14-15). Once again, the two aspects of mercy, the divine and the human.

- Is it possible to forgive and forget?
- Bergoglio states that Jesus did not build walls and his face is mercy. Is the Church the face of mercy? How might it show itself to be the face of mercy?
- 'Do not judge, and you will not be judged yourselves; do not condemn, and you will not be condemned yourselves; grant pardon, and

you will be pardoned' (Luke 6:37). How do these three elements feature in our daily lives: judging others, condemning others, pardoning others?

Worthy theological treatises on mercy undoubtedly will fill many library shelves; even a simple Google search will quickly provide you with the most inspirational quotes about mercy. But this is not just a bit of academic research. The mercy of God is an active force in our daily lives. Cardinal Basil Hume once said, 'It is harder for many people to believe that God loves them than to believe that he exists.' Not only does God love us, God shows us mercy. 'God, be merciful to me, a sinner' (Luke 18:13) is the prayer of the wretched sinner who is exalted by God the Father.

But mercy is not a one-way street, it is not just a gift from God bestowed on those who repent, and there the story ends. The human side of mercy calls on us to be merciful to those around us. Just as we might get asked whether we are more like the elder or younger son (or even the father) in the parable of the prodigal son, so the same can be applied to the parable of the unforgiving servant in chapter 18 of Matthew's gospel. The dramatic story is simple: a servant with significant debts is freed from those debts by the merciful king, who felt sorry for him after he had pleaded for time to pay the debts in full. So the plan to sell the servant, his wife, his children and his possessions was cancelled. On the way out, that same servant met someone who owed him a paltry amount. He demanded his money and began to throttle him. This servant, too, promised to pay the debt over time, but to no avail. He was thrown into prison until he should pay the debt. This whole saga was reported back to the king, who summoned the servant to whom he had shown such great mercy: '"You wicked servant, I cancelled all that debt of yours when you appealed to me. Were you not bound, then, to have pity on your fellow-servant just as I had pity on you?" And in his anger the master handed him over to the torturers till he should pay all his debt. And that is how my heavenly Father will deal with you unless you each forgive your brother and sister from your heart"' (Matt. 18:32-35).

Forgiveness is one of the most difficult aspects of day-to-day life. Here we are not talking about the ability to forgive someone who, perhaps, takes from the fridge a bit of food or a bottle of wine which clearly has your name on it, or forgiving children who might accidentally break a window when playing football (for which mum and dad forgave us many times!). Perhaps we can all think of situations where we have found it really difficult to forgive someone, maybe not even succeeded in doing so. *The Two Popes* actually presents the viewer with a factual situation: two Jesuits, Fr Francisco Jalics and Fr Orlando Yorio, who had both taught Bergoglio in the course of his formation, worked in a shanty town on the outskirts of Buenos Aires, an area known only by the name, or rather, the number given it by the city bureaucracy: Slum 1.11.14. On 23 May 1976 they were kidnapped by naval storm troops. Three days previously they had had their licences to say Mass withdrawn by the Archbishop of Buenos Aires, Juan Carlos Aramburu, who had been told by Jorge Mario Bergoglio that the two were no longer members of the Jesuit community. While this is a very simplistic account of a matter which is far more complex than a brief chronology, it provides some context to whatever is clearly gnawing away at Bergoglio in *The Two Popes*. And what about forgiveness? 'Pride obscured my judgement. The right to say Mass was removed and with it the protection of the Church. I was supposed to protect them … I failed,' says Bergoglio in the film, clearly regretting his actions. Fr Orlando Yorio died of a heart attack in 2000 after suffering for many years from post-traumatic stress disorder. Who knows if he ever forgave

Jorge Mario Bergoglio for what he believed to be an act of betrayal? That same year, Fr Francisco Jalics and his former superior met in Germany, a scene portrayed in *The Two Popes*. 'We cried in each other's arms,' Bergoglio tells Benedict XVI. 'He forgave me.'

- Can true mercy ever be a one-way street?
- 'Mercy is the dynamite that blows down walls,' Bergoglio tells Benedict XVI. This wonderful image suggests that with forgiveness the landscape has changed forever. How true is that?
- In *The Two Popes* Bergoglio and Fr Jalics are shown exchanging the sign of peace at Mass in a gesture which is not just a perfunctory meaningless shake of hands. What do the words 'Let us offer each other a sign of peace' really mean?

Forgiveness is not just a tool to get peace of mind. In a speech in Rome in March 2020 Pope Francis noted that the Beatitude 'Blessed are the merciful, for they shall receive mercy' (Matt. 5:7) is the only one where the cause and the fruit of the beatitude – mercy – coincide: those who show mercy will find mercy. Of course, this is easier said than done.

There are two things that cannot be separated: forgiveness granted and forgiveness received. However, many people struggle; they cannot forgive. Often the harm received is so great that being able to forgive feels like climbing a very high mountain: an enormous effort; and one thinks: it cannot be done, this cannot be done.[25]

This very dilemma is one of the seven petitions contained in the Lord's Prayer, the 'summary of the whole gospel'.[26] I remember in 2007 an online satirical Christian magazine ran a competition to re-write the Lord's Prayer for trendy texting on mobile phones, perhaps an attempt to modernise this age-old message. The aim was to reduce it from the usual 372 characters to 160 characters or less. The winning entry reduced forgiveness to '4giv r sins lyk we 4giv uvaz.' The competition was undoubtedly laudable and even aroused a modicum of media interest, but no matter how many characters we might use, no matter how many times we might say the prayer each day, the message remains the same: the life of every Christian must be one which is characterised by the mercy shown to others. There is no Christianity without mercy.

[25] Pope Francis, General Audience, 18 March 2020.
[26] *Catechism of the Catholic Church*, 2761.

'Who am I to judge?' said Pope Francis. Basil Hume used to tell the story of a priest who began his homily at a funeral by saying he was going to preach about judgement, a statement greeted with dismay. 'Judgement,' he said, 'is whispering into the ear of a merciful and compassionate God the story of my life which I had never been able to tell. It is a very great encouragement to think of being in the presence of a God who is both merciful and full of compassion, because God knows me through and through and understands me far better than I could ever know and understand myself, or anyone else. Only he can make sense of my confused and rambling story.'[27]

Prayer

Lord, be merciful to me a sinner, for only you truly understand the rambling story of my life. May I receive your forgiveness with an open heart, that it may transform my life and make me a bearer of forgiveness to those around me.

[27]   Cardinal Basil Hume, *The Mystery of Love* (London, Darton, Longman & Todd, 2000) p. 87-88.

Further reflection

Dear Brothers and Sisters!
The evangelising mission of the Church
is essentially the announcement of God's
> *love, mercy, and forgiveness*
revealed to mankind through the life, death,
> *and resurrection*
of Jesus Christ our Lord.
It is the proclamation of the good news that
> *God loves us*
and wants all people united in his loving
> *mercy,*
he forgives us, and asks us to forgive others
> *even for the greatest offenses.*
This is the Word of reconciliation entrusted to
> *us because, as Saint Paul says,*
'God was reconciling the world to himself in
> *Christ*
not counting their trespasses against them
and entrusting to us the message of
> *reconciliation.' (2 Cor. 5:19)*

John Paul II, Message for World Mission Day, 2002

$\mathcal{L}$oneliness

Watch Cardinal Bergoglio and Pope Benedict XVI talking in the Chamber of Tears, and Cardinal Bergoglio hearing the confession of Pope Benedict XVI.

> (1 hour 37 minutes into the film,
> a 7-minute scene)

> 'I cannot play this role anymore. Since I was a child, as a boy, I always felt his presence with me at my side. For my entire life I have been alone, but never lonely, until now.'

> **Pope Benedict XVI**

A participant at a February 2020 conference in the Vatican organised by the Pontifical Academy for Life chose to stay in the Domus Santcae Marthae and afterwards wrote an article in the Italian press about papal life in the hotel where Pope Francis has chosen to live: 'A discreet bedroom and meals together: how Pope Francis lives'[28] was

---

[28] The article in Italian written by Arnaldo Casali can be found here: https://www.tpi.it/esteri/papa-frances-co-santa-marta-come-vive-20200302557583/

the headline. 'Obviously, it is a place accessible only to high-ranking prelates, Vatican guests and employees of the Holy See,' wrote the participant in the Vatican conference. 'When the pope comes in or goes out anyone within a thirty-metre radius has to stand aside, taking photos is strictly forbidden and just to get there you have to go through at least five check-points ... For anyone not working in the Vatican the only permit is the key to your own room, which, however, can't be copied since each key has an engraving of a view of the Basilica.'

Domus Sanctae Marthae was built in 1996 and with 106 suites and 22 single rooms it houses Vatican officials, guests, and some employees – who all have to move out for papal elections since the cardinal-electors take over the entire building, and hence its nickname Conclave Hotel.[29]

Some news reports said that when he was shown around the papal apartments in the Apostolic Palace Pope Francis said, 'You could fit 300 people in here!' So he chose to live in Domus Sanctae Marthae, not just because he thought the papal apartments to be too luxurious, but because he needed company, he thrived on company. Soon

---

[29] The previous building on the site, the St Martha Hospice, in the Second World War housed refugees, Jews, and ambassadors from countries who had severed diplomatic relations with Italy.

after his election, stories began to emerge about acts of kindness shown by the pope in his new residence. *The Two Popes* ends with a scene where the Swiss Guard on duty in the corridor outside the pope's room uses his mobile phone to book a flight online for the pope. The real Pope Francis, who has room 201 on the second floor, is said to have got up one morning and when he went out of his room found a Swiss Guard standing in the corridor on duty. In the ensuing conversation the Guard admitted that he had been there all night and, when asked if he was tired, simply replied, 'It's my duty, Your Holiness. I should watch for your safety.' At that point Pope Francis went back into his room and came out with a chair: 'At least sit down and rest,' he said. 'Holy Father, forgive me,' came the reply, 'but I cannot. The regulations do not allow that. Orders from my captain.' The pope smiled, 'Really? Well I'm the pope and I order you to sit down.' Pope Francis then went back into his room and a few minutes later came out carrying a bread roll with jam. 'You must be hungry after all those hours on your feet,' Pope Francis said. 'Bon appetit.'

Who knows if this story is fact or fiction, even though it was well-reported on social media in April 2013. Another story recounts that a young cardinal was in the lift in Domus Sanctae Marthae when

Pope Francis got in. 'Holy Father,' the cardinal said. 'Holy Son,' came the quick reply. Like everyone else at Domus Sanctae Marthae, Pope Francis gets his own coffee from the machine and eats in the refectory with everyone else and not at a separate table. So it seems the man in suite 201 tries to lead as normal a life as possible.

- A palace adorned with old frescos and sculptures or a six-storey residence with a hotel-like entrance, plain marble floors adorned with nice potted plants: where would you feel most comfortable?
- What turns a house into a home?
- Is it possible to be busy and lonely?

Do popes really lead a lonely life? Is the papacy something of a lonely burden as indicated by Pope Benedict in *The Two Popes*? In an interview with Mexican TV in 2015, Pope Francis said that one of the things he would really like to do was to go out for a pizza without being recognised. No chance of that, and I suspect Vatican security might not be overjoyed at the sight of a pizza delivery on a bike, either!

When they were elected, the lives of both Benedict XVI and Francis changed in an instant and took them down a path they neither expected nor wanted: in April 2005 the 78-year-old Cardinal Ratzinger was looking forward to retirement; in March 2013 the 76-year-old Cardinal Bergoglio even had his return ticket to Buenos Aires in his pocket ready to go home and plan his retirement. However, their new roles as servant of the servants of God, shepherd of a flock of over 1 billion Catholics, and Head of the Vatican City State meant that each day would quickly be filled with meetings of all sorts, seeing people every day. But just being busy does not mean that you will never be lonely.

Today it is estimated that more than 5 billion people have mobile devices and the average Facebook user has 338 'Friends'. In the UK people spend an average of 3 hours and 23 minutes a day on mobile devices. Have you ever been walking along the pavement and someone busy texting almost bumps into you (or maybe you're the one doing the texting and you bump into someone)? Now there is even a word for such people: 'Petextrians'. And yet the signs of isolation and loneliness are all too plain to see. In a society with such modern, rapid means of communication how can there be such isolation and loneliness? The phrase 'consumer society' is often used to describe the world we live in today. It is a society characterised by following the latest trend, where consumption decides what is important and anything that is not useful or satisfying can be thrown away. The result, Pope Francis said in an address to bishops in Philadelphia in September 2015, is that at the root of society '... is a kind of impoverishment born of a widespread and radical sense of loneliness. Running after the latest fad, accumulating "friends" on one of the social networks, we get caught up in what contemporary society has to offer. Loneliness with fear of commitment in a limitless effort to feel recognised.'[30] This need to be recognised, the need to fit in with the right friends, can bring with it, Pope Francis intimated, a culture of loneliness. Young people can be especially vulnerable in trying to fulfil a desire to create a cool identity, to fit in with the crowd. It has been said that one of the worst things you can do to a young person is to 'Un-Friend' them on social media. While this may say a lot about modern understandings of friendship, it also reveals the power of a click of a button, resulting, possibly, in painful, damaging loneliness. This is the loneliness of not-fitting-in, not being part of the 'in' crowd. Being 'on-line' is not the same as being acknowledged, respected and loved.

[30]   Pope Francis, Meeting with Bishops taking part in the World Meeting of Families, Philadelphia, 27 September 2015.

LONELINESS

Loneliness can take other forms, too. There is the loneliness of an elderly widow or widower, who, after many years of happy married life now finds themselves alone, surrounded, as the cliché says, only by their memories. A text is often read at funerals which says:

> Death is nothing at all.
> I have only slipped away to the next room.
> I am I and you are you,
> and the old life that we lived so fondly together
> is untouched, unchanged.
> Whatever we were to each other, that we are
> still.
> Call me by the old familiar name.
> ... Laugh as we always laughed at the little
> jokes that we enjoyed together
> ... Why should I be out of mind because I am
> out of sight?[31]

In *The Two Popes* Benedict XVI is not talking about the loneliness of physical isolation. He says that he has been alone all his life, but only now feels

---

[31] Although the text is often read as a poem, it was actually part of a sermon delivered in 1910 by Henry Scott-Holland (1847-1918), priest at St Paul's Cathedral, London, while the body of King Edward VII was lying in state in Westminster.

lonely. 'I lack company', he says, 'always alone.' Bergoglio attempts to provide solace by referring to the prophet Isaiah, 'Do not be afraid, for I am with you' (41:10), but Benedict XVI responds: 'I know he's here but he doesn't laugh. At least I don't hear him laughing.'

- What are the differences between a 'Friend' on social media and a true friend?
- How would you describe a culture of loneliness among young people?
- How would you describe the loneliness of old people?

The Two Popes is a film, not a true factual account, but a few thoughts come to mind: Benedict XVI is an elderly man who has led a busy life, in which, especially in recent years, every moment of every day has been accounted for. He has been surrounded largely by personal aides and other staff, and he has now taken a momentous decision to change, to step away from it all. There is the loneliness of the decision-making, the loneliness of the unknown of the future. On his last day as pope, the real Benedict XVI said: 'I am no longer the Supreme Pontiff of the Catholic Church, or I will be until 8.00 p.m. this evening and then no longer. I am simply a pilgrim beginning the last leg of his pilgrimage on this earth.'[32]

In *The Two Popes* Bergoglio, too, hints at the loneliness of not hearing God's voice. As a young Jesuit he is seen celebrating Mass in a simple country chapel, talking about how TV needs a signal via an aerial and sometimes the signal is bad. 'It's the same when we pray. Sometimes the signal God sends is strong and clear,' he says. 'It works fine. One feels the connection, that we are really plugged in, in direct contact. But other days, one can only say "Well, at least I tried." But you've got nothing back. You don't have an answer. You say, "Father, that doesn't happen to you." People believe that, for us, it's different, that we have a direct line with God. No, it's not like that. For us, it's the same as for you. What I mean is today I'm not worthy of delivering a sermon. My words would be empty.'

There is perhaps a common thread running through all of this: ultimately, loneliness is the inability to experience the presence of God. The recently-bereaved widow or widower, Benedict XVI as portrayed in *The Two Popes*, the young Bergoglio who has lost the connection with God, the young person who placed their trust in social

[32] Pope Benedict XVI, Address to the faithful of the diocese of Albano, 28 February 2013.

media friendship, may all feel an emptiness, even a sense of betrayal. When the pilgrim can no longer see the road ahead, or hear the voice of God, then the glorious journey may certainly seem a lonely one. Loneliness is not simply a physical condition, for neither Pope Benedict XVI nor Pope Francis or indeed anyone in such a position could be said to be physically alone. *The Two Popes* portrays the loneliness which is a sense of emptiness.

A simple adaptation of a phrase from the French theologian Blaise Pascal (1623-1662) says that within each one of us there is a space that only God can fill.[33] Before they entered the Promised Land, Moses said to the people of Israel: 'Be strong, stand firm, have no fear, do not be afraid of them, for the Lord your God is going with you; he will not fail you or desert you' (Deut. 31:6). The pilgrim is never alone, for God does indeed fill the space in the heart that only God can fill. The challenge of faith is to hold on to this truth, in the darkest moments of life, to realise that our hearts are not empty, but God is there.

[33] '... there was once in man a true happiness, of which all that now remains is the empty print and trace. This he tries in vain to fill with everything around him, seeking in things that are not here the help he cannot find in those that are, though none can help, since this infinite abyss can be filled only with an infinite and immutable object; in other words by God himself'. Blaise Pascal, *Pensées* (New York, Penguin Books, 1966), p. 75.

Loneliness, suffering, death can all make us think that we have been abandoned by God, that God has forgotten us. Speaking in Rome in 2016 Pope Francis reminded pilgrims of God's everlasting love: 'The Lord is faithful, he does not leave one to despair. God loves with boundless love, which not even sin can restrain, and thanks to him the heart of man is filled with joy and consolation.'[34]

Sometimes, joy and consolation may seem somewhat distant. My mum spent the last three weeks of her life in a home where she received wonderful care and attention from devoted staff. Family and friends spent many happy hours in her company before she died late one Friday night. I remember going into her room next morning and, even though I knew she had been happy there and had died peacefully, I was overcome by a surge of loneliness. Since that day, with my lovely wife and fantastic brothers, sister, nephews and nieces we have many times celebrated that wonderful lady who was our mum, mother-in-law, and granny. Loneliness is something that we are all likely to experience at some stage in our lives. Be strong; stand firm; the Lord will not desert us.

One of the fears about loneliness can be that fear of losing family and friends and hence subsequent isolation. 'I don't want to be on my

34   Pope Francis, General Audience, 16 March 2016.

own,' is a phrase heard all too often. 'Father of orphans, defender of widows: such is God in his holy place. God gives the desolate a home to dwell in' (Psalm 68:6). This lovely image from the Psalms tells us that God himself provides in a special way for the lonely by welcoming them into his own family. Loneliness is not in the divine vocabulary.

- Can you think of times when you have seen or experienced the depths of sheer loneliness?
- 'The most terrible poverty is loneliness, and the feeling of being unloved.' What do you think of this statement by Saint Teresa of Calcutta?
- What can help in times of loneliness: neighbours, God, prayer, the Church?

The year 2020 has also brought with it the loneliness and isolation caused by the coronavirus pandemic, with many countries in lockdown and a clear message: 'Stay at home'. There has even been speculation that one of the effects of the pandemic might be that people begin to think that being alone is good for you, that the only truly healthy lifestyle is the solitary one, staying at home and keeping other people away. Church worship has become digital with services via live-streaming. Whereas in the past anyone could go to church, now there is a minimum requirement: access to the internet and a decent broadband speed!

But there is something missing: community. The coronavirus pandemic has seen a great community spirit flourishing in many areas and in many ways, with community WhatsApp groups, quizzes, shopping deliveries and so on, all positive ways to overcome isolation and loneliness. With its new emphasis on effective digital worship, a challenge for the Church is to ensure that community is not lost, a note struck by Pope Francis himself preaching at one of his own televised Masses after Easter. The pope was reflecting on familiarity with the Lord and stated that the familiarity of Christians 'is always communal. Yes, it is intimate, it is personal, but in community. A familiarity without community, a familiarity without the Church, without the people, without the sacraments is dangerous.' An unnamed bishop had written to the pope to criticise him for celebrating Easter in the huge, cavernous St Peter's Basilica with no one present. At first the pope wondered what the bishop was talking about, but then understood the danger he was hinting at: 'He was saying to me: "Be careful not to 'make viral' the Church, not to 'make viral' the sacraments, not to 'make viral' the people of

God. The Church, the sacraments, the people of God are concrete".'[35]

We are social animals living in community. Our faith is not dependent, one hopes, on broadband speed! The apostles experienced familiarity with the Lord in the concreteness of daily life and then spread the good news throughout their communities. We, too, are called to be ambassadors of the good news, and in the challenging circumstances of today ensure that loneliness does not dwell in our communities.

Prayer

Lord, you provide a home for the lonely, your unfailing love is always with us, for only you can truly fill the heart of all those whom you hold in your embrace. Be with all those who today feel emptiness and isolation, and may your light dispel the darkness of despair.

[35] Pope Francis, Homily at Mass at Domus Sanctae Marthae, 17 April 2020.

Further reflection

When we have our back to the wall,
when we find ourselves at a dead end,
with no light and no way of escape,
when it seems that God himself is not
    responding,
we should remember that we are not alone.
Jesus experienced total abandonment
in a situation he had never before
    experienced
in order to be one with us in everything.
He did it for me, for you, for all of us; he did it
    to say to us:
'Do not be afraid, you are not alone.
I experienced all your desolation in order to
    be ever close to you'.
Today, in the tragedy of a pandemic,
in the face of the many false securities that
    have now crumbled,
in the face of so many hopes betrayed,
in the sense of abandonment that weighs
    upon our hearts,
Jesus says to each one of us:
'Courage, open your heart to my love.
You will feel the consolation of God who
    sustains you'.

Pope Francis, 5 April 2020

Love

Watch Jorge Mario Bergoglio's choice between the young woman to whom is he about to propose and the call to be a priest.

(38 minutes into the film, an 8-minute scene)

'You will have to learn to love her in another way.'

Fr Jalics

Love may be 'a many-splendored thing', to borrow the title of a 1955 film, but it is also a very complex thing. It is not sloppy romance (although that might have been involved along the way), but one of the most fundamental of human needs. Love is at the heart of human life.

In planning a wedding ceremony in church, couples are usually asked to choose from a selection of Scripture readings appropriate for the celebration. Rarely chosen is that passage from the Song of Songs 'The voice of my love! See how he comes leaping on the mountains, bounding over the hills. My love is like a gazelle ...' (S. of S. 2:8-9). Maybe no grooms see themselves as gazelles!

The most popular reading is very well-known:

Love is patient; love is kind; love is not jealous; love is not boastful, or puffed up or rude; it does not insist on its rights, it does not take offence, it does not plan evil, it does not rejoice at wrongdoing but rejoices in the truth. It puts up with everything, it believes everything, it hopes everything, endures everything. Love never falls away' (1 Cor. 13:4-8).

It might seem strange to reflect on love through the cinematic lens of *The Two Popes*, which is certainly not about the dilemma of choosing appropriate Scripture passages for a wedding. Interestingly, part of Bergoglio's story as recounted in the film is about having to make a choice between his girlfriend and a vocation to the priesthood. According to an account given by Bergoglio himself, he was preparing to celebrate Student Day, a September holiday, by having a picnic with friends. His sister, Maria Elena, has said that her 17-year-old brother was planning to propose to one of the girls at the picnic. But for no obvious reason Bergoglio visited the local church and went to confession and was inspired by the spirituality of the priest. He never went to the picnic but went home instead. Four years later, he entered the seminary.

In a dramatic black-and-white flashback, *The Two Popes* shows Jorge Mario trying to give flowers to the young lady to whom he has just revealed his conviction that his calling lies elsewhere. In the March 2013 media frenzy to uncover every bit of papal tittle-tattle, the headlines uncovered a somewhat different story about the pubescent crush of a 12-year-old: '"The Pope fancied me – and he said if I wasn't keen he'd become a priest," former sweetheart says'; 'Spurned in puppy love, Bergoglio turned to the Church'; 'Pope Francis and Amalia Damonte – a match not made in heaven'. Speaking to the media just after Bergoglio's election to the papacy, 77-year-old Amalia said she and Jorge Bergoglio were both 12-years-old when he told her 'If I can't marry you, I'll become a priest'. 'Luckily for him,' Amalia told the media, 'I said no!'

But without trying to sort out fact from fiction, in *The Two Popes* a young Bergoglio is seen arriving in the Jesuit seminary and acknowledging that he knows to what he is saying 'No' and that she has a name. The profound reply – ironically from the same Fr Jalics whom the film later suggests may have been betrayed by Bergoglio – could be addressed to every human being: 'Love has many faces. It's a big mistake to think one can live without love.'

Basil Hume put it a bit more bluntly:

Always think of God as your lover. Therefore he wants to be with you, just as a lover wants to be with the beloved. He wants your attention, as every lover wants the attention of the beloved. He wants to listen to you, as every lover wants to hear the voice of the beloved. If you turn to me and ask, 'Are you in love with God?' I would pause, hesitate and say, 'I am not certain. But of one thing I *am* certain – that he is in love with me.[36]

- 'Love has many faces. You will have to learn to love in her another way.' What do you think Fr Jalics means?
- How many kinds of love have you experienced in your life?
- Have there been times when you have been absolutely certain that God loves you?

[36] Basil Hume, *The Mystery of Love* (London, Darton Longman & Todd, 2000), p. 24.

LOVE

The phrase perhaps used most frequently in talking about God's love for us is 'unconditional love.' But in our daily lives we're probably more likely to hear something along the lines of 'You scratch my back, I'll scratch yours'. Ironically, the origin of this phrase about doing someone a favour in the expectation of getting a favour in return lies in corporal punishment in the navy in seventeenth-century England. Punishments for a variety of serious offences included being tied to the mast of the ship and flogged with the whip known as the cat o' nine tails by a member of the crew. Demonstrating perhaps a sense of mercy, love, or just plain cunning, crew members were known to reach agreements to give each other just slight lashes with the whip – just 'scratching' the offender's back – so as to ensure that they might get off lightly if they were in the same position. Nowadays, it would probably be called strategic planning!

So how can something be given unconditionally? I remember in the mid-1980s in Rome when I was working at Vatican Radio being invited, or rather encouraged by some Italian nuns to call in on my way to work at a small family-run bakery found in one of the many narrow side streets leading to the Vatican. As I left at the end of the third or fourth visit, the baker's wife handed me a brown envelope, with instructions to open it when I got to work. It will probably come as no surprise to the reader to learn that I had been given 500,000 lire in cash – about £200 in those days. Such kind donors insisted this was simply a gift ... and the fact that their son would like to work in the Vatican was pure coincidence. In their eyes, it was an unconditional gift!

But God's love is not like that, it is not a gift given to us in the hope of getting something in return.

> The *first step* that God takes towards us is that of a love that anticipates and is unconditional. God is the first to love. God does not love because there is something in us that engenders love. God loves us because he himself *is love,* and, by its very nature, love tends to spread and give itself. God does not even condition his benevolence on our conversion. If anything, this is a consequence of God's love ... God loved us even when we were wrong.[37]

The enormity of this can be both difficult to grasp and humbling: God loves *me.* Such an unconditional

---

[37] Pope Francis, General Audience, 14 June 2017.

statement is as true for the pope as for the pauper, for the author as it is for the reader, for God's love is not a vague general love of humankind, but a specific love for each and every individual, each one created in the image and likeness of God. The work colleague I find difficult, the in-law I find impossible, the unbearable politician, the bossy parish priest. Can God really love them all? God loves with the eyes of God, the tender mercy of God's heart, and calls us to do the same.

Before communion at Mass there is the prayer 'Lord, I am not worthy.' Luke's gospel provides the vivid account of the Pharisee and the tax collector at prayer. The former lists all the good deeds which set him apart from the rest of humanity. The despised tax collector simply says, 'God, be merciful to me, a sinner' (Luke 18:9-14). It is the tax collector, Jesus tells us, who 'went home again at rights with God; the other [man] did not.' God's love is unconditional and specific. He doesn't have a closed list of Facebook Friends because God loves everyone, even those I might find it more difficult to love; and if I am loved by God, then I, too, must love in the same way. A call to be like the humble tax-collector, not the Pharisee so full of himself.

I remember an Irish comedian who used to appear regularly on TV in the 1980s. He joked about a Catholic going to heaven and receiving a guided tour from St Peter himself, who pointed out where the good Protestants were, the good Jews, etc., and then they came to a 30ft high wall. 'What's that?' the Catholic asked in a loud voice. 'Sshhh,' said St Peter, 'keep your voice down. The Catholics are in there.' 'But why the wall?' 'Oh well, the Catholics think they're the only ones up here,' came the reply.

In the film documentary *Pope Francis: A Man of His Word*, the pope says

God does not see with His eyes. God sees with His heart. And God's love is the same for each and every person. No matter what your religion is. Even for an atheist it's the same love. When the final day comes and when there's enough light on Earth to see things as they are, we will be in for a surprise! Do you believe that Mahatma Gandhi or Martin Luther King are less loved by God than a priest or a nun? God loves and sees us all with His heart. And maybe that's the only common bond all men have, the bond of God's love. Other than that we are even free not to love him.

- 'Are you envious because I am generous?' says Jesus recounting the parable of the labourers in the vineyard (Matt. 20:1-16). Is it really possible to love everyone?

- How can we show unconditional love in our daily lives?
- Are Mahatma Gandhi or Martin Luther King likely to be in heaven enjoying God's love?

God's love is not like receiving a nicely-wrapped present which ends up gathering dust on a shelf. It is a gift to be used since we are all called to share that love with others, to bring God's love to others.

> We learn from God to seek only what is good and never what is evil. We learn to look at each other not only with our eyes, but with the eyes of God, which is the gaze of Jesus Christ ... Love of God and love of neighbour are inseparable and are mutually related. Jesus did not invent one or the other but revealed that they are essentially a single commandment.[38]

Reading these words of Pope Benedict XVI makes me think of two passages from the Gospels, one from Mark and one from Matthew. In chapter 7 of Mark's gospel, Jesus criticises the Pharisees and scribes for their adherence to the law, putting

[38] Pope Benedict XVI, Angelus address, 4 November 2012

aside the commandment of God in order to cling to human traditions: 'How rightly Isaiah prophesied about you hypocrites, as it is written: "This people honours me with their lips, while their hearts are far from me. They worship me in vain, teaching human commandments as precepts".' (Mark 7:6-7) In Matthew 25 Jesus paints a stark picture of the last judgement which is very clear about the importance and indeed the reward for loving one's neighbour. The virtuous receive their eternal reward in heaven: 'For I was hungry and you gave me food, I was thirsty and you gave me drink, I was a stranger and you welcomed me, needing clothes and you clothed me, sick and you visited me, in prison and you came to see me ... Amen I say to you, in so far as you did this to one of the least of these brothers or sisters of mine, you did it to me' (Matt. 25:35-36, 40). The message could not be clearer: if we truly love God, then the way to demonstrate that can be seen in how we treat others, in how we lead our daily lives.

At one time there were so many Catholics living on the street where our family lived that it was known as 'Pope's Alley'. In the later years of mum's life, long after dad's death and we had all moved away, it was a heavily-populated Muslim area, with virtually no Catholics left on the street. When mum was in hospital, the Muslim neighbour visited her, and when she was at home would regularly bring her food. When we thanked him for all he was doing he looked surprised. 'But she's my neighbour,' was his simple reply. And he was there in the Catholic church at her funeral, too.

Many years ago in leading discussion groups in Catholic parishes I used to enjoy posing the question 'Are Catholics Christians?', to which I would mischievously answer 'No, because they would never allow religion to interfere with their daily lives.' In some of our churches today, the sad reality is that some people leave immediately after Communion. The dismissal at the end of Mass today provides food for thought: 'Go in peace, glorifying the Lord by your life.' That is done not by ending our religious observance at the church door, or by separating out the commandments into what we like and don't like, but by living out the one commandment of love every day: love of God and love of neighbour.

- Can you think of times when love has been shown or come from the least expected quarters? What thoughts do such gestures, actions generate?
- In the drama television series *The New Pope*, John Paul III states that the main problem in the world today is love. 'The question, then,

is how are we to love? This is my way: with tenderness, without passion. My beloved cardinals, perhaps we cannot fully express our faith but we can express our tenderness. It is our hope and our ambition.' Is this Christian love? How do you think this sort of love can be expressed?

- 'Truth may be vital but without love it is unbearable,' Bergoglio tells Benedict XVI just after hearing his confession in *The Two Popes*. What do you think he means?

'No one has greater love than to lay down his life for his friends' (John 15:13). Jesus' words are often seen as the ultimate example of the love which motivates service and self-sacrifice. Maybe it is that sort of sacrifice which has contributed to the loneliness of Pope Benedict XVI depicted in the film. As he notes in a somewhat caustic remark to Bergoglio, 'The Curia's like a machine. You put your hand inside, it chops it into mincemeat. They always defend themselves. Sometimes [it] feels like being pope is to become breakfast.'

In his 2009 encyclical *Caritas in veritate*, Pope Benedict XVI wrote: 'All people feel the interior impulse to love authentically: love and truth never abandon them completely, because these are the vocation planted by God in the heart and mind of every human person'; and again, 'To love someone is to desire that person's good and to take effective steps to secure it.'[39]

If ever there was a message as valid as it is today as it was on the very day it was written, then it must be St Paul's words to the people of Corinth written nearly 2000 years ago, cited at the start of this session. St Paul lists many of the enduring attributes of love. One of the great challenges of being a true Christian living the one commandment of love of God and of neighbour must be to have the desire and ability to replace the noun 'Love' in St Paul's Letter with your own name: always patient and kind; never jealous; neither boastful nor conceited; never rude and never seeks its own advantage; does not take offence or store up grievances; does not rejoice at wrong-doing, but finds joy in the truth; always ready to make allowances, to trust, to hope and to endure whatever comes; Love never comes to an end. For as it says in John's gospel, 'By this everyone will know that you are my disciples if you have love for one another' (John 13:35).

In words from the 2018 documentary film *Pope Francis: A Man of His Word*, which resonate so much today, the pope states:

---

[39] Pope Benedict XVI, *Caritas in Veritate*, 29 June 2009, n. 1 and n.7.

Tenderness is not weakness, it is strength! Tenderness makes us use our eyes to see the other, our ears to hear the other, to listen to the cries of the children, the poor, those who are afraid of the future. To also listen to the silent cry of our common home, our sick and polluted Earth. We have so much to do, and we must do it together. In the darkness of the conflicts we're living through, each of us can become a bright candle to remind us that light will overcome darkness, and never the other way around.

The final word about love goes to the late Cardinal Basil Hume, who, of course, never made it to be pope but who, it is believed, at least got one vote in the very first ballot at the October 1978 conclave which elected Karol Wojtyla who then took the name John Paul II. In 1984, from the comfort of Archbishop's House in London, Basil Hume was watching TV reports of famine in Ethiopia and the harrowing images made such an impression on him that he decided to go and visit the country himself. One day he arrived by helicopter in a particular settlement and when he got out of the helicopter a small boy came up and took him by the hand.

He was aged about nine or ten and had nothing on but a loin cloth. The whole of the time I spent there, that child would not let go of my hand. He had two gestures: with one hand he pointed to his mouth to indicate his need for food; the other was a strange gesture, he took my hand and rubbed it on his cheek.

I realised slowly that he was lost and totally alone – and starving. I have never forgotten that incident and to this day wonder whether that child is alive. I remember when I boarded the helicopter to leave he stood and looked at me reproachfully; an abandoned, starving ten-year-old child.

I appreciated in quite a new way those two profound and fundamental needs – for food and love. With one gesture he showed his need for food, and with the other his need for love. It was much later that day that I realised in a new way the secret of the Eucharist, for the Eucharist is food and love. Taught by that small boy, I saw what the heart of the Eucharist is – his Body and his Blood. For indeed there is no life without food, and no life worth living without love. They are two fundamental requisites for you and me. When he said he wanted us to have life and have it more abundantly, then he must give us his love, and the love he gives is pre-eminently through that sign of his love, the Eucharist.[40]

Prayer

Lord Jesus, you gave us a simple summary of the greatest commandment: to love the Lord your God with all your heart, with all your soul, with all your mind and with all your strength, and to love your neighbour as yourself. Give me your grace and your strength to do as you command.

Further reflection

Jesus taught once and for all
that love for God and love for neighbour are
  inseparable;
moreover, they sustain one another.
Even if set in a sequence, they are two sides
  of a single coin:
experienced together they are a believer's
  strength!
To love God is to live of him and for him, for
  what he is and for what he does.
Therefore, to love God means to invest our
  energies each day
to be his assistants in the unmitigated service

---

[40]   Basil Hume OSB, *Light in the Lord* (Slough, St Paul Publications, 1991), pp. 110-111.

of our neighbour,
in trying to forgive without limitations,
and in cultivating relationships of communion
and fraternity.
God, who is love, created us to love and so
that we can love others
while remaining united with him.
It would be misleading to claim to love our
neighbour without loving God;
and it would also be deceptive to claim to love
God
without loving our neighbour.
The two dimensions of love, for God and for
neighbour,
in their unity characterise the disciple of
Christ.

Pope Francis, 4 November 2018

Epilogue

In one of the early scenes of *The Two Popes* Cardinal Ratzinger is meeting and chatting to cardinals before the conclave that would elect him as pope. He stops to talk to the Brazilian Cardinal Hummes and ends their brief exchange by saying 'Nice to see you.' Next to Cardinal Hummes is Cardinal Bergoglio, whom Ratzinger walks past, barely making eye-contact. 'No "encantado" for you, Jorge,' says Hummes. The final scene of the film shows Pope Francis and Pope Benedict XVI laughing and joking together as they watch the World Cup Final. This is the result of journeying together, listening, confessing, and engaging in fruitful conversation.

On one level, *The Two Popes* is nothing but a 125-minute conversation. It is not about a complicated plot, sub-plot, and some of the other perhaps more traditional elements of many modern films. It is an important and revealing conversation. It is not about conservative v. liberal; old v. new; tradition v. reform. *The Two Popes* highlights the capacity for conversation to build bridges and enable transformation.

It is in the cut-and-thrust of Benedict XVI and Bergoglio talking about change and compromise and the ensuing conversations which culminate in the film's final scene that we discover the heart of the film: that change is not about getting the other person to agree with me, but that what really matters is people's capacity to dialogue and listen, even if they disagree. There is even a religious word for it: communion. *communio?*

Throughout the film, and even among many media professionals writing about the real Pope Francis and Pope Benedict XVI, there is the deliberate portrayal of two very different characters: the traditional German pope and the liberal Argentinian cardinal, with a leaning in many media circles towards the Francisophiles. But *The Two Popes* demonstrates that one of the greatest of human gifts is the humility to accept that my role in life is not to change the other at all costs, to get the listener to agree with me, but to acknowledge that it is possible to listen, to talk, to respect and love even though the views that are held are different. What unites Pope Benedict XVI and Bergoglio is the glorious journey on which God has called them. It is not their role to change the route, since Jesus is the Way. That journey, just like it does for all of us, provides opportunities to consider each other as human beings and be open to listening, reflecting, sharing, and being in dialogue.

That real relationship of dialogue between Pope Francis and Pope Benedict XVI was highlighted by Pope Francis as he spoke to journalists on the flight back from Armenia in June 2016:

> I have gone to see [Pope Benedict] many times, or spoken with him by telephone ... The other day he wrote me a little letter – he still signs with that signature of his – with good wishes for this trip. Once – not just once but on several occasions – I have said that it is a grace to have a wise 'grandfather' at home. I say it in front of him and he laughs. For he is the Pope emeritus, the one who watches my back with his prayers. I never forget the talk he gave to us Cardinals that 28 February: 'One of you certainly will be my successor. *I promise my obedience*'. And he did. Then I heard – I don't know if this is true – I stress that I heard this and it may be gossip, but it sounds like him, that some people have gone there to lament about 'this new Pope ...' and he has sent them packing! In the best Bavarian style, politely, but he sent them packing. If it isn't

true, it is a good story, because he is like that. He is a man of his word, an upright, a completely upright man! The Pope emeritus ... He is very intelligent and for me he is the wise grandfather in the house.[41]

On 13 March 2013, from the balcony of St Peter's Basilica, Pope Francis spoke about the start of 'a journey of fraternity, of love, of trust among us. Let us always pray for one another. Let us pray for the whole world, that there may be a spirit of great fraternity.'

At the end of *The Glorious Journey*, please pray for those who may have journeyed with you, for those who are close to you. In the documentary film *Pope Francis: A Man of His Word*, the pope says: 'To us Christians the future has a name. And its name is Hope. It's the virtue of a heart that doesn't lock itself up, that doesn't dwell on the past, and not only survives the present, but is able to see a tomorrow.'

Pope Francis went on to say that after Morning Prayer each day he recites St Thomas More's 'Prayer for Good Humour'. May it guide and sustain us as we travel the glorious journey on which Christ has not only called us but accompanies us each day:

[41] In-flight press conference of Pope Francis from Armenia to Rome, 26 June 2016.

EPILOGUE

Grant me, O Lord, good digestion, and also
*   something to digest.*
Grant me a healthy body, and the necessary
*   good humour to maintain it.*
Grant me a simple soul that knows to
*   treasure all that is good*
and that doesn't frighten easily at the sight
*   of evil,*
but rather finds the means to put things back
*   in their place.*
Give me a soul that knows not boredom,
grumblings, sighs, and laments,
nor excess of stress, because of that
obstructing thing called 'I.'
Grant me, O Lord, a sense of good humour.
Allow me the grace to be able to take a joke
to discover in life a bit of joy,
and to be able to share it with others.

References

All Scripture texts are taken from *Revised New Jerusalem Bible Study Edition*, Darton, Longman and Todd, London, 2019.